Dare to Believe Again

motivated, and excited about the many possibilities that God may have for you as you pursue His plan for your life. I encourage you to read it.

—**Kay Arthur,** Best-selling Author, International Speaker, Co-Founder, Precept Ministries International

Have you ever felt like you've made too many mistakes and God will never use you? Do you think change isn't possible? You're not alone! Countless people give up but shouldn't. There are answers to these questions and much, much more in this power-packed book, *Dare to Believe Again.* It's a *must read* for anyone who desires to believe again and live their dreams.

—**Dr. Thelma Wells (Mama T),** Founder, A Woman of God Ministries & Generation Love-Divine Explosion, Professor, Speaker, Author (Formerly core Speaker for Women of Faith Conferences)

Have you experienced the death of a dream? Whether you've lost sight of a dream or you are daring to dream again for a different life, it's important for you to *believe again* that it is possible. Kathleen Hardaway gives positive encouragement and practical ways to overcoming obstacles in living out your dreams. In her latest book, *Dare to Believe Again,* her personal and insightful way of writing helps you to courageously step out in faith and move forward toward a life you never dreamed possible.

—**Karol Ladd**, CEO, Engage Parenting, Bestselling Author, National Speaker

Dare to
Believe Again

Boldly Live Out Your God-Given Dreams

Kathleen Hardaway

NASHVILLE

NEW YORK • MELBOURNE • VANCOUVER

Dare to Believe Again
Boldly Live Out Your God-Given Dreams

Published in New York, New York, by Morgan James Publishing. Morgan James and The Entrepreneurial Publisher are trademarks of Morgan James, LLC. www.MorganJamesPublishing.com

The Morgan James Speakers Group can bring authors to your live event. For more information or to book an event visit The Morgan James Speakers Group at www.TheMorganJamesSpeakersGroup.com.

Unless otherwise noted, all quoted Scripture is from the New American Standard Bible (1995).

ISBN 978-1-68350-371-2 paperback
ISBN 978-1-68350-372-9 eBook
Library of Congress Control Number:
2016919674

Cover Design by:
Rachel Lopez
www.r2cdesign.com

Interior Design by:
Bonnie Bushman
The Whole Caboodle Graphic Design

In an effort to support local communities, raise awareness and funds, Morgan James Publishing donates a percentage of all book sales for the life of each book to Habitat for Humanity Peninsula and Greater Williamsburg.

Get involved today! Visit
www.MorganJamesBuilds.com

Contents

Foreword

Do you have a *dream* in your heart but you're not sure how to achieve it? I believe God has divinely placed this book in your hands, and it wasn't by accident that this book and title captured your attention.

Dare to Believe Again: Boldly Live Out Your God-Given Dream is a wonderful title for this book! What makes it even more *wonder-filled* is that the content of this book helps deliver what you need in order to fulfill your God-given dreams!

Dare to Believe Again is what you should do when life can be so full of disappointment. Maybe you've given up or lost hope that you will ever live out your dreams. This is why Kathleen has written this tremendous book, and she gives you specific steps that will help you reach your dreams.

As I have traveled throughout the U.S. and many places around the world, it's remarkable to see the joy on the faces of people who are using their God-given gifts. And God wants to do the same with you.

No matter your age, your education, or your financial situation, it's still God's plan that you know your gifts and learn how to walk in them (1 Corinthians 12:1).

Dare to Believe Again is an easy read which will help encourage you to fulfill God's call on your life. This book is filled with practicalities and inspiring stories of people who pressed on in spite of their difficulties and setbacks. However, what gives it even greater value is Kathleen's life. Her story will inspire and encourage you to keep on keeping on, no matter what life brings.

The last chapter gives the reader specific directions on how to "Soar Again." If you've never soared, this book will help you get out of the chicken coop and be what God intends you to be. It will help you mount up with wings like eagles (Isaiah 40:30-31).

As you read this book you will be encouraged, inspired, motivated, and excited about the many possibilities that God may have for you as you pursue His plan for your life.

May the Lord use this book to greatly help you live the life God created you to live! *Dare to Believe Again*!

—**Kay Arthur**, Co-founder, Precept Ministries International

Shooting for the Stars

What do you want to be when you grow up? Were you ever asked that question when you were a kid? There were no boundaries; you could shoot for the stars, as they say, and no one could stop you.

The grownups around you might have encouraged you and said, "Do you want to be a fireman, a nurse, a pilot, a teacher, a musician, a baseball player, a doctor, a lawyer, a mom, an engineer? You name it—you can be *whatever* you want to be." Ever heard that? I did.

Are you still *shooting for the stars,* or did your dreams get lost in paying the bills and living life? Did you grow up and somewhere along the way your dreams seemed to have passed you by? Do you ever feel like you're on a treadmill and you're doing the same thing over and over again? If so, you are not alone. Countless people are unhappy with their jobs.

"Eighty-six percent of the employees polled said they planned to actively look for a new position in the upcoming year. Another 8% said they may do so and are already networking. Only 5% intend to stay in their current position."[1]

People are looking for a change, but what many are really looking for is *contentment*. The demands of this life can often cause you to live at such a fast and furious pace that it's easy not to stop and take an aerial view of your life. It's hard to really see *how* you're living or *what* you're really living for.

Did it occur to you why the movie *Gravity* might have done so well, winning seven Academy Awards? If you didn't see the movie, the film is set during fictitious space shuttle mission STS-157. Dr. Ryan Stone (Sandra Bullock) is a medical engineer aboard the *Explorer* for her first space shuttle mission. Her companion is veteran astronaut Matt Kowalski (George Clooney), commanding his final expedition.[2]

"The story, written by Cuaron and his son Jonas, is very simple and straightforward: How will the two surviving team members of a crippled American space shuttle contrive to get back to Earth before their oxygen runs out?"[3]

Matt Kowalski, unfortunately, doesn't make it. The majority of the movie is simply Dr. Ryan Stone, a space capsule, and space (the galaxy). Sandra Bullock does an outstanding job capturing the emotions of someone who goes from being fascinated with the wonder of God's creation to wondering how she is ever going to return home. As she is suspended in space, she is forced to think about her life. When she reflects about the routine and normalcy of her past life, it seems she wants to believe that there has to be more to life.

Clearly, most of us won't experience a space shuttle, galaxy experience; yet everyone should slow down long enough to take a strong overview of their lives and consider how they're living.

Maybe you've accomplished some amazing things; and yet, at this point in your life, you feel *stuck*. You feel powerless in your current situation. There's an overwhelming cloud that covers you, and you wonder, *Is this it? Will my life ever be any different?* The thought of having your same life is causing you great anguish, and you wonder how anything could ever change.

What is it that runs deep in your soul? Do you have an ongoing nagging in your heart that simply will not go away? Maybe you've shared your dreams with family and friends and just talking about it brings tears to your eyes. You know you were made for more, but you're just not sure how to get there.

Over and over again, as I talk to people about their dreams, it often brings about deep emotions. Their pain is real because it is possible they are not using their gifts for God's glory.

Maybe you've heard some of the incredible stories of people who have ended up living on the street due to hard, gut-wrenching circumstances, yet they are enormously gifted—an artist, a writer, a musician. Their talent is still within them, and it must come out. There they are sitting on a sidewalk, some playing amazingly beautiful music, while others are painting beautiful pictures. It's God-given, it's within them to play and to paint. Nothing can explain it, except it's God-given, and it's simply miraculous!

What brings you to tears? What burns in your heart? What dream would you live if money or time weren't an issue? It's my passion to give you steps to help take you toward your God-given dreams, no matter what obstacles you face.

What do you want to be when you grow up? Unfortunately, America has placed more importance on what you do rather than who you are becoming. In this book, we're going to look at who God created you to be.

As you read and study, you will learn principles that will help you dream big. Stop and think of yourself suspended in space for just a

Chapter 1

When Your Dream Fades

Believe Again

You are never too old to set another goal or to dream a new dream.
—C. S. Lewis

*D*id you stay up late night after night studying in college? When I was in school, everyone seemed to have their own method of studying. Many of my friends needed solitude and silence. I just needed help—and in a big way.

I was happy to be with anyone who would help cram the answers into my head. In those days, there were no Starbucks or the many assortments of great coffee shops. Yes, we would go to the Waffle House! Thinking about it now it sounds a bit funny, but we needed a place that would stay open *all night long*.

I had crazy study habits. Can you relate? I would pull many all-nighters, pop the NoDoz® pills, and study, study, study. I wasn't one for popping any kind of pills; but if I was desperate enough, I might take one because the caffeine helped keep me awake! All I knew was one thing: I had to pass the countless tests that happened while I was in school. I hated tests—all of them. But I didn't have a choice. When it came to getting my college degree, I studied—like it or not.

I had a greater goal than passing tests. Ultimately I desired graduating from college, getting my BA degree, and becoming a teacher. Yes, I had a dream!

What about you, do you have a dream? Are you living it; or somewhere along the way, did life happen and possibly your dreams were hidden among the laundry, the work, and paying the bills?

Are you one of the countless Americans who dislike their jobs? I fully believe Satan is smiling. Often when people are unhappy in their workplace, they are unhappy most any place.

Your job can often consume your life. How tragic if millions of people who are dissatisfied in their careers are simply living for the weekends and for a few vacations a year. An alarming Gallup poll survey found 70% either hate their jobs or are completely disengaged at their workplace.[4] Tragic, isn't it?

When life carries you along, one day you will probably look in the mirror and think, What has happened to my life? You may wonder, How did I get here? This is not at all what you had planned or what you thought your life would look like. Often, if too much time passes by, you could begin to live like this anonymous writer:

First I was dying to finish school and start college.
And then I was dying to finish college and start work.

And then I was dying to marry and have children.

And then I was dying for my children to grow old enough so I could return to work.

And then I was dying to retire.

And now I am dying…and suddenly I realized I forgot to live.

—Anonymous

Can you relate to any of this? It's easy to begin to think that tomorrow will be better than today, but then one day you wake up and wonder how so much time has gone by. What about today? Is there a continual nudging in your heart for change? God may be calling you toward something different in your life, but how are you going to get there?

Maybe you've had so much disappointment in your life that you're just trying to survive, let alone dream any dreams. It's hard to think past your present situation. I have learned that amidst the pain and frustration can be a great time to seek God for what He might be calling you to do.

Do you remember the first time God moved in your life? Often, if you're in a dry desert season in life when nothing seems to be going right and you've had one let down after another, it's time to reflect on the good things God has done for you. Consider making a list of some of the milestones in your life. It's important to reflect on His goodness.

If you're in the midst of tremendous trials, this may be a hard thing to do. The immediate pain can be all-consuming. For sure, it's difficult to believe God again in a storm; but this can also be one of the most important times *to remember* how God has carried you, covered you, and comforted you.

I love Psalm 143:5-6:

I remember the days of old;
I meditate on all that you have done;
I ponder the work of your hands.
I stretch out my hands to you;
my soul thirsts for you like a parched land.
—Psalm 143:5-6, ESV

Stop and truly consider all that God has done. Don't forget, but remember. God tells us to do this for a reason. Make this practical. This is an important step toward believing that God has a purpose and a plan when often you can't see it.

God has used Jeremiah 29:11 in my life countless times, and I still cling to it when life doesn't go as planned: "'For I know the plans I have for you,' declares to the Lord, 'plans for welfare and not calamity, plans to prosper you, to give you a future and a hope.'"

Do you see a key repeated word in this tiny little verse? Plans! Among the chaos that may surround your life, God still has a *plan* and a *purpose*. He may be allowing the trials in your life to get your attention.

Life is not easy. I understand. I've had many disappointments, many hurtful trials, and many frustrations that have been excruciating. There were times I didn't understand, and I wondered why God was allowing such pain in my life. But with each new trial, I knew I had a choice: *dare to believe God again* in the midst of disappointment, or run to the world for answers. What will you choose? The world's answers will often have you running away from God, and it can come in the form of chasing your dreams. Beware!

There are countless books, seminars, podcasts, webcasts, and YouTube videos that teach people how to live their dreams. You can read, hear, and see an abundant number of amazing stories of people who became billionaires, people who climbed Mount Everest, who swam the English Channel, sailed the seven seas. The list is long of the myriad ways people have lived their dreams.

I love reading their stories. They're amazing people who have accomplished incredible and fascinating things. But the stories I'm *most* intrigued with are the "David and Goliath" stories: the stories of people who have dared to believe God again, and again, and again—and they didn't give up. They didn't give up on God and the dream He had placed in their hearts.

I'm most impressed with the people whose lives have impacted our world *for eternity*. Whether they stand on a stage and sing or run like the wind, the people who understand their calling know that it is God who is giving them strength and power to do what they do. They're living for His glory, not their own. They're more concerned about people knowing the name of Jesus Christ than about people knowing their own name. They're sold out for Christ, not sold out for fame. When you meet them, you know. When you see them, it's obvious. They're Christ-centered, not self-centered. You can see the difference.

"God's ultimate plan for your life reaches beyond the visions he's given you for your family, business, ministry, and finances. He has positioned you in your culture as a singular point of light. A beacon in a world that desperately needs to see something divine, something that is clearly not of this world.

"Above and beyond the achievements associated with your vision, he wants to draw people to himself. Our visions are means to a greater end. Namely, the glory of God and the salvation of men and women. This is His ultimate objective, His ultimate desire."[5] Our purpose is to glorify God.

A man who so visibly portrayed this character and purpose was Eric Liddell. There's a reason *Chariots of Fire* was nominated for seven Academy Awards and won four, including Best Picture and Best Screenplay. The

British historical drama film is a fact-based story of runners who ran in the 1924 Olympics. Eric was a devout Scottish Christian who ran for the glory of God.[6]

There is a famous quote from the movie that has become widely popular: "I believe God made me for a purpose. But He also made me fast. And when I run, I feel His pleasure."[7] This statement depicts Eric's life perfectly. He was a man who knew God had gifted him to run, but who also knew that later in life he would become a missionary.

Eric's strong Christian convictions caused him to become the Olympian who would not run on Sunday. Amazing, isn't it? I believe we're still talking about Eric today, *not* because he won a Gold Medal, but because of his great faith and strong beliefs.

Contrast his life with Harold Abrahams, another runner in the movie. There's a scene in the movie where Harold is talking to another runner, Aubrey. Harold says to him, "You, Aubrey, are my most complete man. You're brave, compassionate, kind: a content man. That is your secret, contentment; I am 24 and I've never known it. I'm forever in pursuit and I don't even know what I am chasing."[8]

What a powerful contrast to Eric Liddell's life! Eric knew God had made him fast, but he also knew he was called to be a missionary in China. Eric believed God for both.

I think about the millions of people in our world who are doing the exact same thing: forever in pursuit without knowing what they're chasing. People are desperately trying to fill the void, the empty vacuum in their lives. All the fame, money, beauty, power, family, and friends can't fill it.

I have enjoyed watching Barbara Walters interview many Hollywood stars. So many appear to have it all; but often, if you listen long enough, they say in so many words, *"I'm still looking for more."*

A relationship with the Lord Jesus Christ is the only thing that will ever give you true joy and lasting contentment. I like the way the Amplified Bible explains 1 Timothy 6:6-7. It says,

> [And it is, indeed, a source of immense profit, for] godliness accompanied with contentment (that contentment which is a sense of inward sufficiency) is great *and* abundant gain. For we brought nothing into the world, and *obviously* we cannot take anything out of the world.

"Get busy living or get busy dying!" This quote from the movie *The Shawshank Redemption* is certainly an interesting quote. I don't want to tell someone to get busy dying, but the fact remains, we're all going to die. How can you get busy living? By pursuing godliness. If that's your life's ambition, you will have complete contentment—the contentment that Harold Abrahams looked for so desperately.

What about you? How's it going? What are you chasing? Are you content? Do you feel more like Eric—a man who walked with God and followed His path—or like Harold Abrahams—chasing dreams, but still no contentment?

> And He was saying to *them* all, "If anyone wishes to come after Me, he must deny himself, and take up his cross daily and follow Me."
> **—Luke 9:23**

Maybe you know Christ and have walked with Him many years, but the constant waves of disappointments have come into your life over and over again, and you're about to throw in the towel. Do you need to believe again? God is whispering in your heart, "BELIEVE! Don't give up. TRUST Me! Don't back down and shut down." What is it you do that makes you feel God's pleasure? He delights when His children use the gifts and talents He has created them to use.

Oh my friend, before you can press forward, you need to decide and determine in your heart that daily you will believe God again and again. This is the *first step* toward living an amazing *audacious* life.

Step One: Believe Again

1. Do you know when you surrendered your life to Christ?

2. Did your life change?

3. Are you discouraged and feel like giving up?

4. Will you determine to *Believe Again* that Christ has a plan and purpose in your life?

5. Make a list of some of the things you know God has done in your life and begin trusting Him again for your future.

6. Don't give up; believe again!

Prayer: God, I'm tired of living like I have been living. I give You my life. I give You my hurt, my pain, my bitterness, my anger; and I lay it at Your feet. Today is a brand new day. Help me believe that You have a plan, that You have a purpose even when I can't see it. I'm completely Yours; help me see *Your* dreams for my life, not mine. I praise You. Amen!

Chapter 2

Feeling Like a Failure?

Stand Again

Many of life's failures are people who did not realize how close they were to success when they gave up.

—Thomas Edison

will never forget the day I heard Mary Kay Beard tell her story. I couldn't believe what I was hearing. She began by telling the audience that it was never her plan to hold a gun in the face of any bank teller and say to them, "Give me your money." She also never imagined she would have the nerve to do this many times. These are words actors say while playing the role in a movie; this couldn't be something anyone actually did!

As a young woman, Mary Kay Beard let the pain and anger from an abusive childhood drive her into a life of crime and danger. By the time she was twenty-seven she was wanted by both state and federal authorities and was the target of a mafia contract. Finally, captured, convicted of armed robbery, sentenced to twenty-one years, and thrown into solitary confinement in an Alabama prison, Mary Kay took stock of her life.

Mary Kay began to read the Bible in prison. She started a personal relationship with God, and her life turned around completely. After being paroled, Mary Kay accepted Prison Fellowship's challenge to become its first Alabama state director in 1982. One of her assignments was to create a Christmas program for inmates.

At one of her speaking engagements, a conversation with an ex-prisoner's daughter solidified the program's focus. "What about the inmates' kids?" the woman asked. "They are the real victims." Mary Kay recalled the toiletries that prisoners gave their children on Christmas. So she and a crew of volunteers began creating a program to provide clothes and toys for prisoners' children.

Their plan was to erect a Christmas tree at Birmingham's Brookwood Mall, encouraging shoppers to buy presents for specific children. Then someone suggested writing the children's names on paper ornaments shaped like angels, creating an Angel Tree! Mary Kay helped cut out one hundred paper angel ornaments and then visited prisoners to invite them to sign up their children.

"God never wastes anything," Mary Kay says. "He used my own criminal past to give me credibility in their eyes. And they trusted us."[9]

Today Angel Tree Ministries that Mary Kay Beard launched in 1982 has reached millions of prisoners' children with the love of Christ.[10]

What an amazing story of a woman who could have lost hope; instead, she focused on what God could do in her life, rather than on her dreadful circumstances. She could have checked out on ever having any joy back in her life. Instead, she clung to a God who brings wholeness to the downcast, healing to the hurting, and purpose for the one who will believe that even in the worst circumstances, *God is there*. He can use you for good if you let Him.

Have you ever purchased a Christmas gift for Angel Tree Ministries? I have, and who would have thought it started with a woman who dared to believe God would forgive her for armed robbery? Mary Kay Beard dared to believe God *again* for her dreams!

I love Mary Kay's story. No matter how far you've fallen or how much you feel like a failure, God can use all the broken pieces of your past for His glory. What's your story? Do you feel like you've blown it far too many times for God to ever use you? Do you wonder how in the world God can take all the mistakes, all the messes you may have made in your life, and use it? He can!

Oh my friend, not only can He use all the broken pieces, He can radically restore and give you a life you never dreamed possible. There's nothing He doesn't forgive. There's nothing He can't wipe clean.

Think about Peter, one of Jesus' twelve apostles. Peter was a man who, at times, made quick, rash decisions. Imagine having been with Jesus, seeing the miracles of Jesus, hearing the teachings of Jesus and yet, under pressure, denying you knew Him. Peter denied He knew Christ, not once, not twice, but three times. He had three times to change his mind. Yep, he blew it! Oh, but his story wasn't at all over!

Peter became a man whose proclamation would later be used to start the church of Jesus Christ. Jesus had asked the disciples who they said He was.

Simon Peter answered, "You are the Christ, the Son of the living God." Jesus replied, "Blessed are you, Simon son of Jonah, for this was not revealed to you by man, but by my Father in

heaven. And I tell you that you are Peter, and on this rock I will build my church, and the gates of Hades will not overcome it."
—Matthew 16:16-18, NIV

Think of that for a minute. Even though he had earlier denied Jesus three times, Peter was used in such a powerful way! At the end of his life he died for Christ; yet in the beginning of his walk with Him, Peter had denied Him. What a contrast, what a change, what a story!

Have you made wrong choices in the heat of the moment? Was it under the influence of family and friends that maybe you made choices you regret?

Far too many think that following God's Word and His precepts is ridiculous, unimportant, and irrelevant. Unfortunately, they do not realize that God's ways are *always best* until the ripple effects of their sin get their attention.

The Bible even says that sin is fun for a season, and then the grave consequences follow.

By faith Moses, when he had grown up, refused to be called the son of Pharaoh's daughter, choosing rather to endure ill-treatment with the people of God than to enjoy the passing pleasures of sin.
—Hebrews 11:24-25

Adultery often causes divorce; pornography can shatter marriages; alcohol destroys countless lives; drugs dash the dreams of many; lust, greed, and selfishness bring heartbreak.

Will God forgive these kinds of sins? Absolutely! "If we confess our sins, he is faithful and just to forgive us our sins and to cleanse us from all unrighteousness" (1 John 1:9, ESV). Is there any sin He won't forgive? No!

Do you feel like a failure? I have many times. Maybe you don't feel smart enough or educated enough to live your dreams. I understand. I will never forget standing on the stage in Ontario, Canada, speaking to a crowd of women and thinking, *How did I get here?* I looked back and realized it was one step, one day, one month, one year at a time, trusting God to open the doors for the dreams He placed in my heart to come true.

My dreams are being lived out daily as I step out by faith and believe God for the open doors that only He can open. Through man's eyes it would be impossible, but with God all things are possible (Matthew 19:26). However, it hasn't been an easy journey.

Looking back to my college days, I certainly wasn't encouraged by my teachers to pursue a life of speaking or writing. I would tell my speech teacher that I really was interested in speaking. It didn't matter what I said to him, he encouraged me in a different direction. *"Drama?"* he would say, "Do you like the theater?" Yep, I had lots of drama all right, but it wasn't in a drama class. A major problem with that career— who can remember all those lines for a play? Nope, the theater and acting wasn't for me!

It was the week of finals, and I'll never forget the day I was giving my last speech for that speech class. I stood on a large stage in front of my class peers and my professor. The only notes we could use had to be written on 3x5 index cards. With all of my other tests that week, I had put off really preparing for my final speech. Trying to *wing* a twenty-five-minute speech was a huge, horrific, humbling mistake. Trust me, don't try it! There I was—mumbling, trying to figure out what I going to say next. I had my cue cards, but I had one major problem—they were out of order.

My classmates started to laugh, my teacher looked concerned, and I was freaking out! I stood there shuffling my cards thinking, What am I supposed to say next? I kept looking through my cards. It was becoming a nightmare, and I wondered how I was going to get through the speech. *Horribly* was how!

The way I ended my college speech class was laughable, only I wasn't laughing. I believe I made a D on the speech, but I deserved worse! F for failure is how I felt, yep! School has always been difficult for me. With a touch of ADD, sitting still and focusing was a problem.

The year I was trying to complete my degree and obtain my teaching certificate was the year they decided that teachers were graduating without learning the basic courses every teacher should know and, therefore, would be required to take a test. Their English, writing, math, and science skills were all a bit fuzzy. Remember the term "fuzzy math"? Well, that was happening with certified teachers. And it was about to happen with me!

I was not happy that I had another major test. If I didn't pass this one, I might not get my teaching certificate. Yep, I failed the first one. They gave me one more stab at it. At that point I got a *team of tutors*. I barely passed—but I passed! Years later, my classmates must have been in shock when they read and saw that I was a published author and speaker! Always remember, God is bigger and greater than the academic world!

I learned that it's important not to let what happened to you in your school life influence what God may have created you to do today! When you've been laughed at and you feel stupid or not as educated as many around you, cling to the One who created you in His image (Genesis 1:27). Remember, God is there when you feel like a failure.

Don't let the harsh, hurtful words and insults from teachers, family, or friends stop you from doing what God is calling you to do. Forgive them and move on. It's not easy—I understand—but it's so rewarding when you know that God is doing His work through you no matter your past.

Stand when you feel like crawling. Throughout Scripture we see God telling His people *to stand.*

> Then the LORD said to Moses, "Rise up early in the morning and stand before Pharaoh and say to him, 'Thus says the LORD, the God of the Hebrews, "Let My people go, that they may serve Me."'"
>
> **—Exodus 9:13**

Imagine how Moses must have felt when God asked him to do this. Stand before the King! God may be asking you to stand before men who appear smarter, greater, and mightier. Oh, but you know that "…greater is He who is in you than he who is in the world" (1 John 4:4).

Moses stood again and again:

> But Moses said to the people, "Do not fear! Stand by and see the salvation of the LORD which He will accomplish for you today; for the Egyptians whom you have seen today, you will never see them again forever."
>
> **—Exodus 14:13**

Moses believed God again. Will you do this?

Believe God, not man. There's a host of people who may not stand with you, but *you keep standing, keep believing in Him—again and again and again.*

We see in Psalm 22:23,

> You who fear the Lord, praise Him;
> All you descendants of Jacob, glorify Him,
> And stand in awe of Him, all you descendants of Israel.

Do you feel like a failure? Stand in awe of Him. Stand in His presence, His power, His divine purpose for your life. Keep standing and watch what God will do!

Time for change! Let go of the past, and move forward toward a greater future in Him.

Step Two: Stand Again

1. Have you ever felt like a failure? What made you feel this way?

2. Are you still holding on to the pain of hurtful words and comments from the past?

3. Ask God to help you stand, to move forward, and to live out what He has called you to do.

4. Daily pray and ask God to be your rock, your source, and your strength when those around you make you feel like a failure.

5. Remember, there is freedom knowing that in Christ no one is a failure.

6. Get back up and stand again, and again, and again.

Prayer: God, help me let go of the past and help me look to You for my future. Sometimes the hurtful words that others have said to me still hurt. Lord, I lay them at Your feet. Take all my mistakes and use them for Your glory. I don't want to ever feel like a failure again. I praise You, Lord, for a new beginning. Help me, Lord, to stand again. Amen.

Chapter 3

You Were Made for More

Dream Again

I have a dream!
—Martin Luther King, Jr.

*D*o you feel like your dreams are fading further and further away? Life keeps passing you by, and so do your dreams. You're starting to believe you may have missed it. But you know deep in your soul *you were made for more!*

Satan wants nothing more than for you to become worried, restless, and to make you think your life seems to have no purpose. Don't listen to his lies! He's doing all he can to stop you from living the life God has planned for you.

Satan's goal for your life is to STEAL and KILL and DESTROY you, but Christ came so that you may have LIFE, and have *it* ABUNDANTLY (John 10:10).

How are you doing? Unfortunately, far too many are stressed out, burned out, and are freaking out about their future. It's easy to fall into a life of anxiety!

Stress starts in the mind. "For as he thinks within himself, so he is…" (Proverbs 23:7). Ask yourself, What do I think about? What's stealing my joy and keeping me from pushing forward with my dreams?

Are you consumed with life's problems and challenges so that your mind dwells on negative thinking? Are you anxious about your future? Does the thought of being stuck in your present situation overwhelm you? Do you feel stuck in the way things have always been? Remember, you're not stuck! Press forward and keep going.

Don't believe that change in your life is not possible. Never give up! It's important to believe your story is *not* over. Until you breathe your last breath, it's not over. God has given you more time, time to do even more. The key is to find out what it is He wants you to do. Do you know? If not, ask Him until He shows you—keep asking!

Often people look at success and believe their career should peak at a certain age. Do you think that's true? Let's look at some highly successful people and see what age they were when they made some great accomplishments:

- Thomas Edison was forty-six years old when he invented the light bulb.
- President Reagan was sixty-nine years old when he was elected the President of the United States in 1981.
- Walt Disney was fifty-four years old when he opened Disneyland.
- Colonel Sanders was sixty-five years old when he kicked off the start of his fabulous franchise for Kentucky Fried Chicken.

I love Colonel Sanders's story! He began selling fried chicken from his roadside restaurant in Corbin, Kentucky, during the great depression. He had many setbacks and disappointments along the way, but he kept going.[11] Aren't you glad he didn't say, "I'm too old for this; I had better just retire"?

I have wonderful childhood memories of sitting around the kitchen table, grabbing chicken out of a bucket of KFC and having a family meal. I know my mom had great memories; it was one of those days she didn't have to cook for a family of six! Who doesn't like the Colonel's chicken? His fabulous career just started to explode much later in his life. Remember, you're never too old to birth a new dream. Be careful not to get discouraged.

From the beginning of time Satan started his schemes by sending His fiery darts to the battleground of people's minds (Genesis 3:1-6). He often enjoys saying, "You're stupid, ugly, worthless, useless, helpless, skinny, fat, old, and hopeless." If you think about these kinds of lies for very long, doubt creeps in, depression sets in, and discouragement is on your doorstep. Worry floods your mind. The overwhelming thought of how you're ever going to move forward with your life begins to take over. It's important to understand who's feeding you all these lies.

When you learn to stand, you begin to learn to fight the thoughts you let enter your mind. We read in 2 Corinthians 10:3-6,

> For though we walk in the flesh, we do not war according to the flesh, for the weapons of our warfare are not of the flesh, but divinely powerful for the destruction of fortresses. *We are* destroying speculations and every lofty thing raised up against the knowledge of God, and *we are* taking every thought captive to the obedience of Christ, and we are ready to punish all disobedience, whenever your obedience is complete.

It's critical that we take "every thought captive"! Begin by being careful of what you think and the things you say to yourself.

Start to recognize who you're listening to. Start becoming more aware of your thought processes. Satan desires for you to listen to him. Are you questioning what God has said? Satan begins with convincing you to doubt God and His Word. The enemy's first attack started with this tactic—*in your mind*.

We see Satan's very first fiery dart in Genesis 3:1. He began by persuading Eve to question God:

> Now the serpent was more crafty than any beast of the field which the LORD God had made. And he said to the woman, "Indeed, has God said, 'You shall not eat from any tree of the garden'?"

It's important not to believe Satan's lies. Genesis 3:4-6 says,

> The serpent said to the woman, "You surely will not die! For God knows that in the day you eat from it your eyes will be opened, and you will be like God, knowing good and evil." When the woman saw that the tree was good for food, and that it was a delight to the eyes, and that the tree was desirable to make *one* wise, she took from its fruit and ate; and she gave also to her husband with her, and he ate.

Be very careful when the lies start flooding your mind—recognize where they come from! This is one of Satan's greatest tactics. In John 8:44, Jesus says this about him:

> "You are of *your* father the devil, and you want to do the desires of your father. He was a murderer from the beginning, and

does not stand in the truth because there is no truth in him. Whenever he speaks a lie, he speaks from his own *nature*, for he is a liar and the father of lies."

When the lies start coming, be careful—your dreams can start fading. Begin again to think on God's promises. Cling to His Word. God tells us to mediate on Him and His Word. These are great verses to think on and memorize:

On the glorious splendor of Your majesty
And on Your wonderful works, I will meditate.
—Psalm 145:5

Make me understand the way of Your precepts,
So I will meditate on Your wonders.
—Psalm 119:27

"This book of the law shall not depart from your mouth, but you shall meditate on it day and night, so that you may be careful to do according to all that is written in it; for then you will make your way prosperous, and then you will have success."

—Joshua 1:8

Every minute of every day you're given a choice. How will you choose to think, and what will you choose to believe—TRUTH or LIES?

This is key, hold on to every one of God's promises! How do you do this? *You must know what the Bible says.* How do you hold on to something you don't know or understand?

You must know God's plan, His ways, His purposes for your life; but first you must know Him. This must be your ultimate goal. Your dreams can be wonderful only under His guidance and His plans for your life.

What do you do when your dreams become nightmares? Have others messed up your dreams? Divorce may have caused your dream marriage to dissolve. Your dream children have changed, and now they don't have anything to do with you anymore. Your dream home is in foreclosure, and you've been laid off from what you thought was your dream job. Millions have had their world rocked by shattered dreams.

Despite the horrific pain and horrible loss, do you dare to believe God again? Yes, believe again when your life isn't at all that you thought it would be. When you only seem to be breathing but not doing much living, *believe again!*

I truly understand broken dreams. From a very young age I always dreamed of being married and having children. Isn't this what most young girls dream about? I just needed to grow up, fall in love, and get married, right? That was my dream.

In some ways it feels like yesterday when I was in grade school. Yes, boys, boys, boys—that's what I thought about and talked about! My girlfriends and I would say, "Who do you like?" "Not sure. Who do *you* like?" On and on we would chat about *the boys.*

If we thought someone had a boyfriend, we began singing the little song, "Johnny and Betsy sitting in a tree, K-I-S-S-I-N-G. First comes love, then comes marriage, then comes Betsy with a baby carriage." Yep, that's what we sang! My life started early with my boyfriends. I would send my handwritten note across the classroom to the cutest guy in the class, or so I thought. "Do you like me? Check yes or no" They liked me! Having boyfriends was never a problem. It didn't end in grade school. No sir, it went right into junior high, high school and college! Dates, dances, and decisions about who I would go out with and what I would wear were about all I worried about. I loved my life, and I thought I loved my boyfriends! But, the song "Puppy Love" comes to mind!

I thought I was in love all right, but I didn't have a clue. The boys I dated believed they were also in love. I still have some of the love letters and cards from those days. One of the cards says, "I will always love you, I will always love you, I will always love you, I will always love you." This was written on the card over sixteen times! I was crazy in love with being in love. Can you relate?

In my first book, *I Kissed a Lot of Frogs, but the Prince Hasn't Come,* I go into great detail about my life and how I have walked the journey of being single. Looking back now, I know why I enjoyed the young romances so much—I wanted to be loved. Deep within the soul of every human heart is a desire to be loved. This is who we are and how God made us.

During these critical days in my life, I received a handwritten note from my father. I didn't realize it at the time, but he was very in tune with where I was in my life. During my freshman year in college, he wrote a short note that has meant so much. He ends the letter by writing,

> I am proud of you in so many ways and I've turned all [4] of you over for guidance, deliverance, help and love. Always remember Jesus through the Holy Spirit is sufficient to handle all problems, especially boy-girl, girl-boy ones. I count on Him for help all the time. Keep going on the *Daily Bread*. We have daily books too that you can have. Hope to see you this weekend. Love and Kisses, Dad

My father knew how to pray. I believe it was through His prayers that my life completely changed. At the age of twenty-one, I surrendered my life to the Lordship of Jesus Christ. It has been an exciting journey since I first believed fully in the death, burial, and resurrection of Jesus Christ (1 Corinthians 15). I have never regretted daring to believe God with my life. It has been a wonderful journey with highs and lows and a lot in between.

Today, I've still never married and I will never have children or grandchildren. I understand staring in a mirror and wondering, Why, God? Why me? What did I do? Why am I so different? What good could possibly come from this? Why?

So, yes, I understand shattered dreams. I understand heartbreak and disappointment and living a life different from the life you had planned. It's been painful, and at times I've been pitiful. BUT, I have dared to believe God again, and again, and again.

I cling to His Word that tells me, "'For My thoughts are not your thoughts, nor are your ways My ways,' declares the LORD" (Isaiah 55:8). I have to believe His ways are best and that He has been directing my steps all along the way. "The steps of a man are established by the LORD, And He delights in his way" (Psalm 37:23). God is the ruler over all, and that means if I'm ever to be married, I will be. But in the meantime, I keep living the dream God has given me today.

I never thought I would be a published author. I'll never forget the day Moody Publishers sent me a contract for my first book. Yes, I was living a dream. But more importantly, God birthed in me more dreams than I ever thought were possible.

People from around the world have emailed and told me that my books and my story have encouraged them greatly. Women have used my books for group Bible studies, retreats, and small groups; mothers, daughters, sisters, families, and friends have used my materials—words that, I believe, God had me write.

I have appeared on national television and radio programs. I've spoken around the country, and all of this has come from a story of broken dreams. Today I love telling people to believe again and dare to dream again, no matter what. It's one of the greatest joys in my life.

So, no matter how different your life looks from what you've planned, God can take all the broken pieces and use it for His glory and His good.

> And we know that God causes all things to work together for good to those who love God, to those who are called according to *His* purpose.
> **—Romans 8:28**

Do you believe this, or are you looking at the people that seem to have it all? Looking at others can be a slippery slope of discouragement. Be careful wishing you had what others have. There are plenty of people you can look to who just might encourage you. If you choose these people carefully, you may be enormously blessed.

I'll never forget the day I saw Nick Vujicic. I was sitting in a packed out crowd of people waiting for him to come on stage. First I heard the sound of an electric motor, and it appeared to be some kind of lift. He was being lifted onto the stage! Then Nick walked out on stage—but not like most of us walk. You see, he has no legs and no arms. I was amazed that he could stand and even walk. Nick's enthusiasm was contagious! I was deeply moved that day, and he clearly made an impact with the audience. I later began to read his books and watch his videos.

I love what Nick says in his book *Life Without Limits*. He writes, "My name is Nick Vujicic (pronounced VOY-a-chich). I am twenty-nine years old. I was born without any limbs, but I am not constrained by my circumstances. I travel the world encouraging millions of people to overcome adversity with faith, hope, love, and courage so that they may pursue their dreams."[12]

He says it all right there. It takes great faith and hope in a God who can do all things, in His love that carries us when we may feel like no one else cares, and the courage to keep on keeping on.

Nick also says, "Often we feel life is unfair. Hard times and tough circumstances can trigger self-doubt and despair. I understand that well. But the Bible says, 'Consider it pure joy, ...whenever you face trials of any kinds.' That is a lesson I struggled many years to learn. I eventually figured it out, and through my experiences I can help you see that most of the hardships we face provide us with opportunities to discover who we are meant to be and what we can share of our gifts to benefit others."[13] What powerful truth Nick speaks! He inspires me greatly.

Who inspires you? Do you have a Nick in your life? You can choose to look at people who seem to have it all or look at those who *rise* above it all. I can't begin to comprehend the challenges that Nick faces daily. But, he's choosing to let God use all the disappointment, all the difficulties in his life, for good.

So what's stopping you? What are you telling yourself and who are you listening to? What obstacles are you facing? Take another step. Today, step toward the vision God has given you! Never give up!

Step Three: Dream Again

1. What is your God-sized dream?

2. What is keeping you from pursuing your dream?

3. How have Satan and others discouraged you?

4. What can you do to begin pursuing your dream?

5. Keep reading God's Word daily. How is He speaking to you about your dreams?

6. Don't ever stop dreaming. Dream again!

Prayer: Lord, I feel discouraged, and I have lost all hope that anything is ever going to change. Help my unbelief. I lay all my dreams at Your feet. I desire Your will above all else. Help my desires to truly be what Your will is for my life. I want to live my life fully as You have planned for me. Take my life and use it for Your kingdom. I'm passionate about making a difference. Amen.

Chapter 4

Courage to Change

Fearless Again

Courage is contagious. When a brave man takes a stand, the spines of others are often stiffened.

—Billy Graham

Flying, dying, snakes, quakes, mistakes—you name it, people are afraid of all kinds of things. Maybe these aren't problems for you, *but* you're terrified to make many changes.

Does change make you feel uncomfortable? Do you often sit in the same seat at church, eat at the same restaurants, go on the same vacations, drive the same roads, have the same friends, and listen to the same music? We are creatures of habit. It's natural and sometimes needful. But, could it be you simply don't like change? Have you wondered why you may feel stuck in your present situation?

Change can be scary, but maybe you would *prefer* to be more of a risk-taker! You can keep feeling comfortable by making the same choices, but is comfort what you're seeking? This is an important consideration! Change can be challenging, but if you're following God's lead, it can be incredibly wonderful. Praise God for the many risk-takers who followed God!

Who comes to mind when you think of a risk-taker? I think of Christopher Columbus. He had an enormous impact in the historical development of the modern Western world. Columbus himself saw his accomplishments primarily in the light of spreading the Christian religion.[14] Did you know that? In grade school I was taught Columbus sailed the ocean blue in1492. I wasn't taught anything about his passion and love for God! He said, "No one should fear to undertake any tasks in the name of our Savior, if it is just and if the intention is purely for His holy service."[15]

Wow! Don't you love that! *"No one should fear,"* he says. But more important than what a great historian says, what does God say? The word *fear* is used 385 times in the Bible. Over and over in Scripture you see that living a life without fear is very important to God. He wants you to live courageously, not in fear. Are you fearful—or fearless?

When I think of someone who had outrageous courage, I think of Todd Beamer. Todd is a man who is remembered by his iconic phrase, Let's roll! Todd Morgan Beamer was one of the heroic passengers aboard United Airlines Flight 93 which was hijacked as part of the September 11 attacks in 2001. Beamer, along with Mark Bingham, Tom Burnett, and Jeremy Glick, formed a plan to take the plane back from the hijackers and led other passengers in this heroic effort. Their courage sparked an historic endeavor that aided in sparing the lives of countless people. They gave their lives for others.[16]

Do you have this same kind of courage? Fortunately, most of us will not experience hijacking, but there are plenty of other situations in life that can cause great fear. If God leads you to step out and possibly change careers, will you? What if He's asking you to move and begin a new church plant? Maybe He's asking you to attend a much smaller church because there you can have a greater impact. What is it that you feel God is leading you to do?

God's calling could very well cause you to step out of your comfort zone. It may not be comfortable or cozy to make a move. We like our La-Z-Boy® chairs with our comfy pillows and our cappuccino in hand. Most of us like our cushy lives and change can be challenging. But—if you have a God-given dream, it's quite possible that God is asking you to get out of the boat. God asked Peter to get out of the boat and come to Him on the water (Matthew 14:29). He may be asking you to do the same thing, and nothing about getting out of boats is typically comfy, and it can be cold!

I remember when I had to get out of a boat; it was the day I learned to water ski. It was a gorgeous day, and I was enjoying being out in the sun and watching my family and friends water ski. I was about fourteen years old and my cousins asked me, "Hey, do you want to ski?" I immediately said, "I've never skied before." "No problem." they replied, "Now is a good time to learn." I thought for a moment— now was not a good time. I was thoroughly enjoying lying on the back of the boat, enjoying the wonderful sun, drinking my Orange Crush", and having fun watching everyone else! "Come on." they kept saying, "It's time." I remember saying something like, "No, maybe a bit later." They responded, "Nope, it's now or never because we will soon be heading back."

This was my moment of decision! Right then I knew I had a choice: would I try it or not? "Okay," I mumbled. "Great, here is your life vest; put it on, and jump in the water." I grabbed the vest and it seemed much

too large. They came over and tightened it just a bit and I didn't think I could breathe! They said, "Now, you don't want it to be too loose. It's important that it not come off." They pulled the straps really tight. Well, being too loose was certainly not a problem now! I thought, *Why is it so important for it not to come off?* I was beginning to get a bit scared and freaked out. This whole thing was way out of my comfort zone!

One thing I knew for sure: I didn't want to get out of the boat or jump into the water. They keep telling me to come on because they didn't have all day. I finally decided to do the slow approach into the water. I went down the ladder on the back of the boat into the freezing cold, murky water. My approach was probably much harder than just jumping in, but I was finally in the water! I had gotten out of the boat!

My cousins starting yelling, "Now this is what you need to do. As the boat begins to take off, grab the rope and let it glide through your hands until you can catch the handle. Be sure and hold onto it. It might pull you a bit, but just hold on. Then sit back and hold both of your skis pointing up with the tips out of the water. Keep holding the tips of your skis up and also keep your arms straight. Don't bend them."

While I was out in the water, which felt like sub-zero, the boats kept zooming by and the waves from the other boats keep splashing water into my face and over my head. Those folks in their big fancy boats seem to be having all the fun! I thought, *This is a big mistake.* Now I wanted out of the water; I wanted to get back in the boat! But, since I had gone to the trouble of getting into the water, I thought I should at least give this thing a try. "Ok, hold on," they shouted. The boat took off and I held on for dear life! I fell forward but keep hanging on! Finally, after drinking half the lake, I let go of the rope, realizing that the face-forward approach was probably not going to get me up!

The next time I held on so long that my arms felt like they were pulled completely out of their sockets and I was about to give up. My cousins encouraged me to keep on trying. Finally, I must have done

something right because suddenly I popped up on top of the water! I couldn't believe it—I was skiing and I loved it! It was an incredible day. Nothing else I had ever done was like it. I skied several more times that day and later learned to slalom-ski. It's still one of my favorite sports!

One thing is certain: if I was ever going to ski, I had to get out of the boat. Nothing about getting out of that boat was fun. Nothing. But, it was worth every bit of the uncomfortable feeling of going from a warm dry boat to cold lake water.

As scared as I was trying to learn to ski, I'm sure it was nothing compared to what Peter was feeling when Jesus asked him to get out of the boat. There's an important lesson God wants us to learn from Peter's walk on the water.

To put Peter's walk in context of the story, we begin in Matthew 14:19-21. We learn in these verses that it had been another miraculous day when Jesus had fed the five thousand.

> Ordering the people to sit down on the grass, He took the five loaves and the two fish, and looking up toward heaven, He blessed *the food*, and breaking the loaves He gave them to the disciples, and the disciples *gave them* to the crowds, and they all ate and were satisfied. They picked up what was left over of the broken pieces, twelve full baskets. There were about five thousand men who ate, besides women and children.

The apostles had just witnessed another miracle, but oh how quickly they forgot the incredible power that Jesus had—but not Peter!

> Immediately He made the disciples get into the boat and go ahead of Him to the other side, while He sent the crowds away. After He had sent the crowds away, He went up on the mountain by Himself to pray; and when it was evening, He

was there alone. But the boat was already a long distance from the land, battered by the waves; for the wind was contrary. And in the fourth watch of the night He came to them, walking on the sea. When the disciples saw Him walking on the sea, they were terrified, and said, "It is a ghost!" And they cried out in fear. But immediately Jesus spoke to them, saying, "Take courage, it is I; do not be afraid." Peter said to Him, "Lord, if it is You, command me to come to You on the water." And He said, "Come!" And Peter got out of the boat, and walked on the water and came toward Jesus.

—**Matthew 14:22-29**

Amazing! At times Peter certainly was impulsive and made some horrific mistakes, but not at this moment. This was not a quick move. He begins by giving us a great principle to live by. Peter said to Him, "'Lord, if it is You, command me to come to You on the water.' And He said, 'Come!' And Peter got out of the boat, and walked on the water and came toward Jesus." (Matthew 14:28-29). No excuses, no complaining, no delays, he got out of the boat; but he first asked Jesus, "'If it is You, command me to come to You on the water.'" He was looking for Jesus, he knew His voice, he believed Jesus would keep him safe, and he was obedient! Imagine Peter crawling out of the boat. The boat was "battered by the waves; for the wind was contrary." It was dark, windy, with waves crashing all around him. But—Peter still would rather risk it all to be closer to Jesus. He got out of the seemingly safe, secure boat to be closer to Jesus. He clearly, at that moment, believed the power of Jesus and that He would keep him from sinking.

Why didn't the other disciples get out of the boat? Instead Peter hears, "It is a ghost." And certainly it's easy to see why they may have thought it was a ghost, but we don't see in Scripture that Peter had

any support from the other disciples. Peter was looking for Jesus, and he wanted to be near Him. It did not matter what the others were doing.

Are you too concerned about what others think about you? Is following Christ unpopular at your work, home, or with your social network of friends? Like Peter, you may be alone in your obedience, but it will be well worth it. Have you ever heard anyone say, "I'm sorry I obeyed God?" I never have. I have never ever heard anyone ever regret being obedient to God. Never.

Do you want God to greatly move in your life? It comes by looking to Him, listening to Him, and then being obedient to Him. Unfortunately, far too many want the miracles, the blessings. They want their dreams to come true but without a surrendered life to Christ. Many want to stay in their boats and still receive God's blessings. This is not the Christian life. This is not the blessed life.

What are you holding on to? What boat are you in? What boat do you think is keeping you from sinking? What is giving you comfort but is holding you back from what God is calling you to? Is it a boat of a wrong relationship that is not honoring to God? Or a boat of financial debt, a boat of alcohol and drugs, a boat of selfish independence? Whatever it is that is holding you back from the Lord, it's time to get out. God is there and He cares. He wants you to step out and follow Him completely.

Once you are out of your boat, there's another important lesson to learn from Peter's walk on the water. Peter did do some water walking, and it was remarkable, but did he mess up? In Matthew 14:30-31 we read, "But seeing the wind, he became frightened, and beginning to sink, he cried out, 'Lord, save me!' Immediately Jesus stretched out His hand and took hold of him, and said to him, 'You of little faith, why did you doubt?'" Peter turned his focus from Jesus to his circumstances, he began to doubt, and he started to sink. Keeping your eyes fixed on the

Lord takes effort, and it's a moment-by-moment choice. We know from Hebrews 12:2, we are to fix our eyes on Jesus. When the frustrations of life come, and they will, don't lose your faith. Believe again. Keep seeking God and His direction and plan.

In your trials and frustrations can you truly walk without fear? Is it really possible? Not only is it possible, but God tells us to live this way. We read in Joshua 1:1-2,

> Now it came about after the death of Moses the servant of the LORD, that the LORD spoke to Joshua the son of Nun, Moses' servant, saying, "Moses My servant is dead; now therefore arise, cross this Jordan, you and all this people, to the land which I am giving to them, to the sons of Israel.

Can you imagine this daunting task? For forty years Moses had led the Israelites through the wilderness. He was a tremendous leader, but now his time had come to an end. It was time for another leader to take his place. God clearly spoke to Joshua about how he was to lead His people. He used a phrase that He wanted him to remember: "*Be strong and courageous*" (Deuteronomy 31:6). And if he didn't understand this the first time, God told him again and again. The phrase *be strong and courageous* is used thirteen times throughout the Bible. How is it really possible to be strong and courageous?

Remember that God is always with you. Deuteronomy 31:6 says, "'Be strong and courageous, do not be afraid or tremble at them, for the LORD your God is the one who goes with you. He will not fail you or forsake you.'"

In Deuteronomy 31:23 we see the phrase again: "Then He commissioned Joshua the son of Nun, and said, 'Be strong and courageous, for you shall bring the sons of Israel into the land which I swore to them, and I will be with you.'"

As you begin stepping out and making changes, there could be days of discouragement when things don't look so good. *Don't be dismayed; God will fight for you.* Over and over you see God winning the battles for His people:

> Joshua then said to them, "Do not fear or be dismayed! Be strong and courageous, for thus the LORD will do to all your enemies with whom you fight."
> **—Joshua 10:25**

> "'The LORD your God who goes before you will Himself fight on your behalf....'"
> **—Deuteronomy 1:30a**

> "'Do not fear, for I am with you;
> Do not anxiously look about you, for I am your God.
> I will strengthen you, surely I will help you
> Surely I will uphold you with My righteous right hand.'"
> **—Isaiah 41:10**

God will fight for you. Do you believe this, or are you living in fear? It's easy to look at your circumstances and become overwhelmed with the challenges that appear impossible to handle. Be careful where you're looking. Family, friends, or co-workers will, at some point, disappoint you. As you begin focusing on your problems, fear and frustration can begin to overwhelm you. You may feel mistreated, misunderstood, and that someone may have manipulated a situation that has caused you harm.

God says, "'Do not fear, for I am with you. *Do not anxiously look about you, for I am your God.* I will strengthen you, surely I will help you, surely I will uphold you with My righteous right hand'" (Isaiah 41:10, italics added).

When you focus on your problems, this is the point at which you begin to sink. It's important to daily determine who you're going to look to and walk with. Will it be the world's solutions, or will you resolve to walk in the strength and power of God Almighty? Always remember where you're looking.

Can you remember days when you were fearless? Were there times in your life you did make changes? God carried you through then, and He will do it again. Do not lose heart. Pray that God will give you the courage to make the changes you need to make in order to follow His call in your life. If He is asking you to get out of the boat, do it.

Believe Him and step out and be fearless again!

Step Four: Fearless Again

1. Are you one who likes to keep doing the same things in your life?

2. Would you rather be comfortable than to make any changes?

3. Think about some times in your life that you were fearless and you know God helped you through the challenge.

4. Do you believe He will help you with your latest fears?

5. What are some changes you feel like God is asking you to make?

6. Is there a sin in your life that is keeping you in the boat and not allowing God to use you?

7. Pray that God will show you how to begin living fearlessly in Him again.

Prayer: Dear Lord, forgive me for not trusting You as I should. Often I try living in my own strength. I confess I have fear at times. I fear failure. I fear the financial markets will crumble. I fear my family will laugh and ridicule my dreams. I fear my faith will be too weak to step out on this new journey. I fear the future. Help my unbelief. Give me Your power to face my fears. Today I will thank You, knowing You are greater than anything or anyone. May I live fearlessly. Amen.

Chapter 5

Don't Give Up

Fight Again

Don't find fault, find a remedy.
—Henry Ford

id you ever say to your parents, "I can't!"? Maybe they encouraged you to ride a bike, dive into a pool, or drive a car. All these things may have seemed a bit scary the first few times you tried to do them. Fear could have overtaken you, but you didn't let it stop you.

Most of your friends rode bikes, swam, and drove cars; so you decided to take the risk and dive into the pool, peddle until your bike kept going, and practice enough behind the wheel of a car until you learned to drive. Then that special day came and you got your driver's license! Remember that fantastic day? Driving a car opened up a whole new world for you. You had a sense of freedom and adventure you never had before. You took a risk and *you didn't give up*.

Imagine our world without automobiles. I'm thankful Henry Ford didn't give up. He said, "Failure is simply the opportunity to begin again, this time more intelligently."[17] Don't you love that? Begin again!

Are you about to *throw in the towel*? That phrase originated from the boxing ring. When a boxer is too beat up to continue, his coach throws the towel into the ring to signal the fight is over. I don't know what it is about boxing movies, but Hollywood continues to put them out.

If you saw the movie *Cinderella Man*, you watched a fantastic story of perseverance in the face of hardship. It's the chronicle of the boxer James J. Braddock, a remarkable account of achievement against all odds. Braddock, dubbed the Cinderella Man, had one of the greatest comebacks in fighting history.

"Here was the amazing architecture of a man's life, existing against the backdrop of one of the darkest periods of our country's history."[18] "You have this man who didn't have money to feed his kids, who had a broken hand, who was never supposed to box again, and he goes on to become the champion of the world, to achieve a greatness no one ever saw coming. That's an amazing fable, even though it's entirely true. You might call it…a classic American story."[19]

There's a powerful scene in the movie where you see one of Jim's boys shivering while lying under blankets on a bed in a tiny bedroom in the back. Jim hears him cough and cough and cough. The electricity had been cut off and his child is extremely sick. At that point, Mae (Renae Zillweger—Jim's wife), folds her hands before her. She closes her eyes, begins to pray. She glances up at her husband Jim (Russell Crowe) as to say why you aren't praying. Jim responds, "I'm all prayed out."[20]

Is that how you feel—all prayed out? You may feel *all prayed out* when God has something so special for you right around the corner.

That's how Jim Braddock felt. Nothing looked good in his life—nothing. But he didn't give up during the times he certainly felt like it. Don't give up and never stop praying!

If you're having difficulty praying, you may want to stop for a moment and pray something like this:

> *God, I feel as though I'm all out of prayers. I come to You today with a broken heart. A heart that needs healing, a heart that wants to sing again, a heart that wants to love again, a heart that wants to laugh again, a heart that wants to be near You again, a heart that wants to believe in You again, a heart that wants to say yes to whatever life You're calling me to. Would You lift my head—would You help me get out of this pit—would You help me believe that You do "…cause all things to work together for good to those who love God…" (Romans 8:28) even though another wave has knocked me down. Give me strength to get back up and to keep walking.*

Daily, moment by moment, keep praying. It's all about God's strength in you and your believing Him to help you through another disappointment. It's about His power working through you.

The apostle Paul wrote,

> And He has said to me, "My grace is sufficient for you, for power is perfected in weakness." Most gladly, therefore, I will rather boast about my weaknesses, so that the power of Christ may dwell in me. Therefore I am well content with weaknesses, with insults, with distresses, with persecutions, with difficulties, for Christ's sake; for when I am weak, then I am strong.
> **—2 Corinthians 12:9, 10**

It isn't about mustering up enough strength to get back up, *but it's asking God to help you to get back up and stand.* When I've been knocked down, there have been times I just wanted to stay down. Can you relate?

When you take the risk and get out of the boat, the last thing you want to happen is for another wave to come and knock you down again. I've been knocked down many times. Disappointment has come in many areas of my life. I've wanted to roll up in a ball, feel sorry for myself, and never get back up. It's been tempting, but where would that get me—a life of pity parties and a life full of regrets!

Oh, I've wanted to quit and give up! How about you? I've seen many who have felt this way. I've watched as friends and colleagues settled into a life that appears comfortable, but deep inside, they're miserable. They stopped taking the risks—they were tired of the waves of disappointment and the knock-out punches that life can bring.

If you feel this way, it's time to get back up and fight again! Are there areas in your life where you feel like you've blown it? Don't give up! God is the God of second chances, third chances, fourth chances…. He never gives up on us, so don't give up on Him. You may feel like throwing in the towel; but your coach, God your Father, is fighting for you and carrying you.

GET UP when life seems hopeless. GET UP when your husband continues to disappoint you. GET UP when your boss is unfair. GET UP when your family drives you crazy. GET UP when you're out of money. GET UP when you've lost your job. GET UP when one more relationship didn't work out and you're sick and tired of being single. GET UP when you don't *feel* like getting up! Don't stay down, but get up and trust God. Get up and believe Him again and again and again.

You may be thinking that fighting doesn't sound too spiritual! Let's look at what God says about that. Nearing the end of his life, Paul says,

> For I am already being poured out as a drink offering, and the time of my departure has come. I have fought the good fight, I have finished the course, I have kept the faith; in the future there is laid up for me the crown of righteousness, which the Lord, the righteous Judge, will award to me on that day; and not only to me, but also to all who have loved His appearing.
>
> **—2 Timothy 4:6-8**

Here Paul describes his life as a fight. He faced many battles throughout his life, but don't you love what he says in the end? "I have kept the faith." This is what you must do. Get back up, stay in the fight, keep the faith, and keep on believing!

Do you hear the lies: you can't, you're stupid, so why keep trying? Keep in mind who whispers those thoughts in your head—Satan. He doesn't want you to stand; he wants you to quit.

> …He was a murderer from the beginning, and does not stand in the truth because there is no truth in him. Whenever he speaks a lie, he speaks from his own *nature*, for he is a liar and the father of lies.
>
> **—John 8:44**

Watch what you're entertaining in your thought processes. Keep it positive. Also, be careful about listening to others' opinions. There always seem to be skeptics around when you're ready to step out and do something that might seem impossible to man. Disappointments will happen. There will be setbacks and possible roadblocks. Keep going; don't give up! I will never forget the first time I heard this simple short story about a mule who decided to step up despite how he was being treated:

Shake It Off and Step Up

A parable is told of a farmer who owned an old mule. The mule fell into the farmer's well. The farmer heard the mule braying, or whatever mules do when they fall into wells.

After carefully assessing the situation, the farmer sympathized with the mule but decided that neither the mule nor the well was worth the trouble of saving. Instead, he called his neighbors together, told them what happened, and enlisted them to help haul dirt to bury the old mule in the well and put him out of his misery.

Initially, the old mule was hysterical! But as the farmer and his neighbors continued shoveling and the dirt hit his back, a thought struck him. It suddenly dawned on him that every time a shovel load of dirt landed on his back, he should shake it off and step up! This he did, blow after blow.

"Shake it off and step up—shake it off and step up—shake it off and step up!" he repeated to encourage himself. No matter how painful the blows or distressing the situation seemed, the old mule fought panic and just kept right on shaking it off and stepping up.

You're right! It wasn't long before the old mule, battered and exhausted, stepped triumphantly over the wall of that well! What seemed like it would bury him, actually blessed him, all because of the manner in which he handled his adversity.

That's life! If we face our problems and respond to them positively and refuse to give in to panic, bitterness, or self-pity, the adversities that come along to bury us usually have within them the potential to benefit and bless us! Remember that forgiveness, faith, prayer, praise, and hope are all excellent ways to "shake it off and step up" out of the wells in which we find ourselves!

There are several things I love about this story. First, there will be things in this life that simply are not fair. People will not always treat you as they should. It's extremely frustrating, isn't it? It's when family, friends, and co-workers don't act as they should that can be some of the most difficult times in life. You must run to Jesus; He is the only one who has perfect, unconditional love. He understands. Remember the way He was treated? He understands.

You run to God first and tell Him how you feel; you lay your burdens at His feet. Get near to God. Then it's time to do your part: step up. You must not stay down when God is telling you to get up. Do you think your situation looks hopeless? I'm sure the paralytic must have thought his life would never change. We see in Scripture, the paralytic had to *get up* and not *give up*:

Being unable to get to Him because of the crowd, they removed the roof above Him; and when they had dug an opening, they let down the pallet on which the paralytic was lying. And Jesus seeing their faith said to the paralytic, "Son, your sins are forgiven." But some of the scribes were sitting there and reasoning in their hearts, "Why does this man speak that way? He is blaspheming; who can forgive sins but God alone?" Immediately Jesus, aware in His spirit that they were reasoning that way within themselves, said to them, "Why are you reasoning about these things in your hearts? Which is easier, to say to the paralytic, 'Your sins are forgiven'; or to say, 'Get up, and pick up your pallet and walk'? But so that you may know that the Son of Man has authority on earth to forgive sins"—He said to the paralytic, "I say to you, get up, pick up your pallet and go home." And he got up and immediately picked up the pallet and went out in the sight of everyone, so that they were all amazed and were glorifying God, saying, "We have never seen anything like this."

—Mark 2:4-12

The scribes were certainly skeptics, weren't they? But Jesus is there in our distresses, diseases, and disappointments, too. In Scripture we often see that Jesus asked others to do their part. He asked the paralytic to "…get up, pick up your pallet and go home." The paralytic must have believed he was healed of his illness; he must have believed he could walk. And those around him certainly believed Jesus could heal him. They went to a lot of trouble to get near Jesus: "Being unable to get to Him because of the crowd, they removed the roof above Him; and when they had dug an opening, they let down the pallet on which the paralytic was lying" (Mark 2:4). We see the paralytic "immediately picked up the pallet." Now that's radical obedience!

What is He asking you to do? Are you following His precepts, His principles? All the dreams and goals in the world are not as important as doing what Christ asks of you. When radical obedience happens, most will be amazed; and the person who is obedient is often the one radically blessed!

In Lysa TerKeurst's book *Radically Obedient, Radically Blessed*, she writes,

Oh dear friend, the call to radical obedience is the fresh invitation your soul is looking for. We all feel a tug at our heart and a stirring in our soul for more, but we are afraid to venture past our comfort zone. Outside our comfort zone, though, is where we experience the true awesomeness of God.

You see we have become so familiar with God yet so unaware of Him. We make the mysterious mundane. We construct careful reasons for our rules and sensible whys for our behavior. All the while, our soul is longing for a richer experience—one that allows us to escape the limits of sight, sound, touch, taste, and smell and journey to a place of wild, wonder, and passion.[21]

Lysa has just described a life that dared to believe again. Are you waiting to get up and walk toward what He's asking you to do?

How near are you getting to God? It's easy to give up if you keep walking in your own strength. Maybe you're trying to get up alone. You may be in church or even teaching a Bible study, but is your distance from God possibly a problem? Are you walking too far from Him? Stop, listen, and look to Him. What's He saying to you? *His power comes as your nearness to Him grows.*

God works in amazing ways as His children follow His call on their lives. Lean in and listen to what He's saying. Don't give up—get up!

Now may the God of hope fill you with all joy and peace in believing, so that you will abound in hope by the power of the Holy Spirit.

—Romans 15:13

Step Five: Fight Again

1. Have you had many setbacks in your life? Don't let them stop you from moving forward.

2. Do you feel like giving up? Don't!

3. Make a list of five reasons you should not quit and give up on your dreams.

4. What principles did you learn from the simple story about the mule?

5. Shake it off, and fight again!

Prayer: Far too often I feel as though I'm in a pit and others are hurting me. You are my strength and my shield. It's my desire to shake it off and step up. Without Your strength and power in my life, it's not possible. Help me daily to keep focused on You and not to let others be a distraction. You are my shield; You are my protector. I praise You today for all that You're doing. Amen.

Chapter 6

Understand How God Made You

Purpose Again

"*...Narrow the road that leads to life, and only a few find it.*"
—Jesus (Matthew 7:14, NIV)

*D*o you know your purpose? Are you excited about getting out of bed every day because you have a higher calling greater than yourself? It's critical to know why you're here.

What reason do you have to live? That's the question that everyone must clearly know and understand. No reason for life; no reason to live. We all need *purpose*, and we need to know our *purpose*.

The world's influences can flood your mind with wrong thinking. It often has you believing that you must be pretty enough, smart enough, talented enough, educated enough, and rich enough to be happy. This simply is not true.

Joy and purpose come as you spend time with Christ and walk in His plan and purpose for your life. Yet, it's easy to want more—more of all the earthly pleasures. In an instant I can easily get pulled into the mindset of wanting more, particularly when I pick up a Pottery Barn catalog! All of sudden I see things and think, I would like to have that. My flesh—our flesh—wants more things, but God desires for us to want more of Him. Are things that you own a problem? No, not as long as they don't own you and you can willingly hold all that you have with an open hand.

So what is it? It's not the world's beliefs and values that give us direction. It's in God's ways, not man's ways. If you truly grasp this, believe it, and walk in it, life has purpose and meaning and you'll want to live as long as possible.

God's greatest desire for your life is for you to have a relationship with Him through Jesus Christ. You get to know Him through knowing His Word, the Bible. Your destiny and life plan will begin unfolding as you daily spend time with Him. Your life will be transformed as you read and study the Bible (Romans 12:1-2). Think about this: are you growing in the knowledge of Him and His Word? If so, your passion will be to please God in all that you say and do, and you will have a desire to live a righteous life.

As a believer, the Holy Spirit living inside you will guide, direct, and give you a desire to follow God with all your heart. Keep praying and seeking His will for your life. His greatest dream for your life is for you to become more like Him. "And we all, with unveiled face, beholding the glory of the Lord, are being transformed into the same image from one degree of glory to another. For this comes from the Lord who is the Spirit" (2 Corinthians 3:18, ESV).

We don't become more like Him and the person He created us to be by *living any way we please*! No, but some have done that and have found themselves behind bars. For a while Bernie Madoff thought he was living the American dream. Here was a man who, for decades, cheated investors out of billions of dollars.[22] Madoff is a perfect example that no matter how much you own, it's never enough.

God is more than enough. Settle this in your heart—believe it! There have been far too many professing Christians who have stood on stages with incredible voices, preached powerful sermons, and have had great notoriety because of their abilities, but have now fallen. There came a point where they didn't walk their talk. The damage was done; and the world points to them and says, "See, you so-called Christians, you are no different from anyone else."

We are *called to be different*, called to walk our talk. Paul said, "Brethren, join in following my example…" (Philippians 3:17). Can you say this? It's not easy. Does it mean you will never sin? No. We know that Christians will sin (1 John 1:8). But, there's a serious problem if you live in habitual sin (1 John 3:4-10). Once you are a believer, sin becomes a choice. Romans 6:11-14 clearly explains this:

> Even so consider yourselves to be dead to sin, but alive to God in Christ Jesus. Therefore do not let sin reign in your mortal body so that you obey its lusts, and do not go on presenting the members of your body to sin *as* instruments of unrighteousness; but present yourselves to God as those alive from the dead, and your members *as* instruments of righteousness to God. For sin shall not be master over you, for you are not under law but under grace.

We're dead to sin and alive in Christ Jesus. We are to radiate Christ and passionately dedicate our lives for the kingdom of God. *This is your purpose.* It's not your popularity that God cares about, it is your character. He says, "...Be ye holy; for I am holy" (1 Peter 1:16, KJV). How's it going for you? You may think it's impossible, but Christ living in you makes this possible!

The world must see Christians as shining lights in this dark and fallen place. Unfortunately, our world is getting darker and darker and darker. We are in a dangerous mess. The language, the lewdness in people's clothing, and the lack of self-control in every area of life should wake us up out of our apathy! It's unbelievable that people are fighting about taking down The Ten Commandments! Shocking that our country has come to this! Our forefathers would not believe how far we have strayed from what they worked so hard to put in place.

Imagine our world if people didn't steal, kill, or covet their neighbor's wife. These commandments alone would change our world! And yet, many think it makes no difference. Oh, it matters. Little by little, God and His Word are being mocked, ridiculed, and lost. That's one reason that every believer is important to the body of Christ.

God says, "Test yourselves *to see* if you are in the faith; examine yourselves! Or do you not recognize this about yourselves, that Jesus Christ is in you—unless indeed you fail the test" (2 Corinthians 13:5). If your desire is not to be a bright light, a witness for Jesus Christ, something is dreadfully wrong. I encourage you to ask God to examine your heart and reveal to you what He sees. Your passion, your dream, ultimately should be for others to see Christ in you.

God created us in His image with gifts, talents, and vision. I love Proverbs 29:18 (KJV) that says, "Where *there is* no vision, the people perish: but he that keepeth the law, happy *is* he." Vision is so important because when your dream fades, so does your passion for life. It's true. If you're not using the gifts God created you for, something in your heart and soul hurts—something is missing. Why do people want to commit suicide? They have lost their purpose, their passion, their reason for life.

In time it can do damage physically. God has gifted each one of us differently to enable us to fulfill His purpose for our lives. For many the quest begins with searching for God's purpose—why God made them.

Years ago it seemed everybody was talking about their personality types! Many wondered and asked themselves, "Am I sanguine, choleric, melancholy, or phlegmatic?" I think it's fun and interesting and has some merit. But, after I figured out that I was mostly sanguine with some choleric, someone said to me, "I think you're an otter." I thought, What in the world does that mean? Now I'm an otter! Later I found out that Dr. Gary Smalley has a personality test that compares people to animals. It's another way to find out about your temperament. You may want to take a look at the Smalley Institute at www.smalley.cc and see his personality test. But whether you're outgoing, demonstrative, determined, easy-going, carefree, childlike, energetic, quiet, fun-loving, helpful, social, sensitive, charismatic, fearful, cheerful, mystical, factual, practical, punctual, imaginative, inventive, creative, or caring, *you are uniquely you*!

Psalm 139:14 (ESV) says, "I praise you, for I am fearfully and wonderfully made. Wonderful are your works; my soul knows it very well." God created every fiber of your being. Have you ever seen a four-year-old child skillfully play a Beethoven sonata or hear a talented cello player play incredible music? Olympians have impeccable skills, doctors have unbelievable minds, and artists are extraordinarily creative. All these things are God-given talents and skills. Don't you see the wonder of God's creation when you see the vast amount of differences among people?

It's amazing to hear the stories from people who knew from an early age exactly what they wanted to do. They knew their talents and they built their lives around those gifts. But using your strengths and talents apart from God is all vanity (Ecclesiastes 1:2-3). The glorious unfolding of your life happens as you use your talent and your skills alongside your spiritual gifts. When a believer is living this way, it's as though all the instruments in an orchestra come together, and it is exactly God's design for your life!

Your abilities and talents all can be used without the help of the Holy Spirit. But spiritual gifts are used through individuals for eternal purposes, for God's kingdom work. It's important for you to understand the difference. He says. "Now concerning spiritual *gifts*, brethren, I do not want you to be unaware" (1 Corinthians 12:1). It's clear that God wants you to know about the gifts and how to walk in them.

Now there are varieties of gifts, but the same Spirit. And there are varieties of ministries, and the same Lord. There are varieties of effects, but the same God who works all things in all *persons*. But to each one is given the manifestation of the Spirit for the common good.

For even as the body is one and yet has many members, and all the members of the body, though they are many, are one body, so also is Christ.
—1 Corinthians 12:4-7, 12

If you are in Christ—if you are a believer in the Lord Jesus Christ—you are part of the body. And if you're not operating as you should within the body, you are weakening the body of Christ. Think about your physical body. If one of your legs is not working properly, how difficult it is for the rest of your body! Have you ever broken your big toe? Ouch! All your toes are important, right? Look at how the text explains this:

For the body is not one member, but many. If the foot says, "Because I am not a hand, I am not *a part* of the body," it is not for this reason any the less *a part* of the body. And if the ear says,

"Because I am not an eye, I am not *a part* of the body," it is not for this reason any the less *a part* of the body. If the whole body were an eye, where would the hearing be? If the whole were hearing, where would the sense of smell be? But now God has placed the members, each one of them, in the body, just as He desired. If they were all one member, where would the body be? But now there are many members, but one body. And the eye cannot say to the hand, "I have no need of you"; or again the head to the feet, "I have no need of you."

—1 Corinthians 12:14-21

These are great verses! Clearly every part of the body is important.

Don't ever feel as though you are less important than anyone else. Don't compare your gifts to others. God has given you the gift/gifts that He has chosen for you. Focus on God and what He has called and gifted you to do, not what He has given others to do. God has chosen you for a purpose and has gifted you for this purpose. He wants to use you. His spiritual gift to you is designed specifically to help you. He desires you to do great things for Him. We see in Ephesians 2:10, "For we are His workmanship, created in Christ Jesus for good works, which God prepared beforehand so that we would walk in them."

If you have never done an in-depth study on spiritual gifts, I encourage you to do so. I did a Precept Upon Precept® Bible study on spiritual gifts, and it was life-changing. There's controversy over some of the gifts, but don't depend on what others tell you. Go to God's Word and see what *He says*. As I dug into God's Word about spiritual gifts, it helped me to become more aware of my own gifts and helped confirm what I was called to do. It is so incredibly freeing! If you haven't done one, I encourage you to do an in-depth study for yourself.

For an overview, read about spiritual gifts in the following Scriptures: Romans 12:3-8; Ephesians 4:11-13; and 1 Corinthians 12:4-31.

Jim Denison does an outstanding job writing about and describing the biblical spiritual gifts. Visit his website, at www.denisonforum.org and see his article, "What Are Spiritual Gifts? How Can I Find Mine?" To do Jim's Spiritual Gifts Analysis, "Find Your Spiritual Gifts," visit his website at http://lovegod.denisonforum.org/strength/394-find-your-spiritual-gifts.

As you read the suggested Scriptures on spiritual gifts that I listed above, did any of the gifts just jump off the page? You may be drawn to several of these gifts. What are you passionate about and where are your interests? You will probably be drawn to the gifts that coincide with these areas.

My spiritual gifts are evangelism, teaching, and exhortation. I'm passionate about encouraging people. That's why I'm writing this book. I want to encourage you! I want to help equip you to do what God has chosen and gifted you to do. I can get very busy doing many things. They may be good things, but I have to stop and ask myself, Is this what I'm called and gifted to do?

Satan can have us busy doing many "good things" but they may not be beneficial to the kingdom of God. When you are walking in your gifts and doing what God has created you to do, you will be so fulfilled and it's fantastic! There's nothing like it.

I love seeing people shine! It's so obvious when the children of God walk in His ways and His purposes. There's a reason Billy Graham has been used so mightily in the lives of countless people. He knew his calling was evangelism. Throughout his life he stayed true to his passion. His ministry, BGEA (Billy Graham Evangelistic Association), clearly states its mission.

God used Billy Graham in my life. In 1979 in Nashville, Tennessee, I attended a Billy Graham Crusade. I will never forget it. As he has in every meeting, Billy gave an invitation. I surrendered my life completely to Christ, and I have never been the same! Soon I had a hunger to know God and His Word. My life changed as I began spending time in Bible study, studying the Bible one book at a time.

I thank God that Kay Arthur stayed true to her gift of teaching. She uses her gifts in her writing and speaking. Precept Ministries International was birthed out of her Inductive Bible Studies, and now this ministry is impacting lives around the world.

When I want to be encouraged, I have often read one of the many books written by the late Zig Ziglar. His gift of encouragement has been used in countless people's lives. When I've really been in a hurry, I've quickly glanced at one of Zig's videos online. Whether it's one of his books, videos, or quotes on Twitter or Facebook, Mr. Ziglar always encourages me.

Here are three gifted individuals who knew their gifts and have walked in what God called them to do. No, not everybody will be a Billy Graham or Kay Arthur or Zig Ziglar, but what about the millions of Sunday school teachers who have helped impact our world? What about those who volunteer to help in whatever way is needed? What about those who visit the sick or lonely simply to show compassion and encouragement? Maybe you love working with children and you are fulfilled by teaching a Sunday school class or staying with the children in the nursery during worship services. That's fantastic! You are desperately needed in the body of Christ!

Your service to the Lord doesn't have to be your full-time job. You may work at a normal forty-hour-a-week job, but you love taking short-term mission trips. You may be able to use your knowledge in the medical field in a remote village in Africa. You may want to encourage the weary, the sick, the poor, or someone God brings along your way who is going through a trial.

There are countless ways Christians can use their gifts for God and His kingdom. Millions of believers are serving God in a myriad of ways at home and around the world. Is it the lost, the sick, the hungry, the poor, the widow, the foster child, the single mom, the uneducated, the disabled, the drug addict, or the alcoholic that you desperately want to help? The list could go on and on with the tremendous needs of people around the globe. We know without a doubt that there are millions of hurting people in our world. That's why it's important that we're all doing our part. Pray and seek God for where you fit into the body of Christ. The key is to know what your gifts are and to know what God has called you to do. It's rare that God gives us the entire picture and plan all at once, so be willing to take one step at a time.

In Stormie Omartian's book *Just Enough Light for the Step I'm On* she writes, "When you hear God telling you to move in a certain direction, let me give you two words of advice: *Do it*! Refusing to walk according to God's leading will get you nowhere. Oh, you will arrive someplace all right, but if it is not where God wants to bless you, it will still be nowhere."[23]

Step by step God will lead you. What is God whispering in your heart? What are you passionate about? Often whatever it is you're passionate about is the place God is directing you to go. Just remember that God's leading is always in accordance with what He says in the Bible.

Imagine using your gifts in the greatest way possible! Imagine really living your dreams! It's God's desire for you to reach as many as possible with the gospel of Jesus Christ. He may have you work with just a few. Jesus spent most of His time with His twelve disciples. But what an impact these men had! They helped changed the world and continue to impact lives through their work.

Step Six: Purpose Again

1. If you haven't done an in-depth Bible study on spiritual gifts, I would encourage you to do one.

2. Take Jim Denison's Spiritual Gifts Analysis at http://lovegod. denisonforum.org/strength/394-find-your-spiritual-gifts.

3. Prayerfully seek God about your gifts. Continue to move toward using the talents and gifts God has given you for His kingdom.

4. What you're passionate about is often what God is calling you to do.

5. Get godly counsel from the spiritual leaders in your life. See what strengths and gifting they see in your life.

6. There are many great Christian Life Coaches available. If you want to work with one, be sure to get references before spending money and time with a person or an organization.

7. Purpose again, and don't give up!

Prayer: Dear Lord, it's my desire to walk in the talents and gifts You have given me. Don't let me go in the wrong direction or pursue areas in which I'm not gifted. I'm passionate for You to direct my path and for You to help me have a clear plan and purpose. Help me as I develop my gifts. My prayer is that I won't take for granted the areas in my life that come easy. Help me work hard in the things that are more difficult. May all that I say and do be for Your glory. Amen.

Chapter 7

The Procrastination Problem

Move Again

If it's important to you, you will find a way. If not, you will find an excuse.

—Unknown

ave you ever thought about why people procrastinate? There are boatloads of books and blogs on the subject. However, without understanding the real problem for procrastination, if you haven't stopped to see what might be holding you back from moving forward, it's difficult to determine how to make life-changing goals. Let's look at it and try to see where you may be on the list of procrastinators.

Procrastination is the practice of carrying out less urgent tasks in preference to more urgent ones, or doing more pleasurable things in place of less pleasurable ones, and thus putting off impending tasks to a later time, sometimes to the "last minute" before the deadline.[24]

Could it be that you're choosing the more pleasurable things? Every day you make choices. If you choose the less important, that nagging ache in your heart continues as you're having the constant challenge of reaching your goals.

The list may be long for how you spend your time and why your life dreams may be taking a back seat. Certainly the urgent tasks must get done. If you have a long commute to work, your workday may average eleven hours. If you have a family, you have little time to call your own. You have little down time and the thought of not having any time to really chill out is overwhelming. What do you do? Have you ever taken a serious look at how you're spending your time and how there might be a window of time you haven't considered using?

It's important to know why you may not be moving forward. People procrastinate for many reasons. Have you discovered why you're possibly putting off the important goals? Think about it for minute. Do you know what's holding you back?

Take a look at some of the top reasons people procrastinate. Do any of these seem familiar?

- Fear
- Laziness
- Lack of direction
- Unable to focus
- Perfectionism
- Overwhelmed

- Unable to make decisions
- Not motivated
- No passion for change
- Lack of purpose

Anything on this list describe you? I have certainly, at one time or another, fallen into some of these things. I love to watch a good movie, and I've wasted tons of time doing so. Certainly there is no problem watching an occasional good, clean movie, but for sure this book and chapter on *procrastination* would have been completed much sooner without my *procrastinating* at times. It's a matter of constant choices that we all make every single day.

What's holding you back? Daily your choices are determining what your future holds. Have you ever thought about the things the Bible says about procrastination? It's interesting. Let's take a look. How does God instruct us to manage our time? We are to seek Him above all else.

1. Seek First His Kingdom

Matthew 6:33-34 says, "But seek first His kingdom and His righteousness, and all these things will be added to you. So do not worry about tomorrow; for tomorrow will care for itself. Each day has enough trouble of its own."

With the overarching demands of the day, your time will pass by quickly. If you choose daily to seek Him first and foremost, giving Him time with prayer and in His Word, you *will* make better choices throughout your day. *He is priority one.*

2. Give Him Your Fears

Don't let the fear of failure or ridicule stop you. Realize that some fear is normal, but press on anyway. Don't let this hinder you, causing you to procrastinate without moving forward toward your God-given dreams.

God tells us not to fear. Deuteronomy 3:22 says, "Do not fear them, for the LORD your God is the one fighting for you." Don't you love that God will fight for you!

I have discussed the problem of fear in detail in Chapter 4. You may want to refer to this chapter if fear is keeping you from moving forward.

3. Choose Not to Be Lazy

I like the way the New Living Translation describes the one who is lazy. "Lazy people want much but get little, but those who work hard will prosper" (Proverbs 13:4).

How I wish I could tell you that I have never been lazy. Not so. I have lain on the couch watching too much TV and made up far too many reasons why I thought I needed the time. Yes, there is a time to rest. We know that God took a day to rest, and we also need time to rest (Genesis 2:2-3). *But* determine if you're truly resting and need it or if you are just being lazy. The book of Proverbs has some great precepts about being lazy.

> The way of the lazy is as a hedge of thorns,
> But the path of the upright is a highway.
> **—Proverbs 15:19**

> Poor is he who works with a negligent hand,
> But the hand of the diligent makes rich.
> **—Proverbs 10:4**

It's important to understand what causes you to be lazy. We're creatures of habit, so this is a critical issue to consider. If it's a problem, begin making changes today.

Whatever you do, do your work heartily, as for the Lord rather than for men, knowing that from the Lord you will receive the reward of the inheritance. It is the Lord Christ whom you serve.

—Colossians 3:23-34

If you are passionately doing what God has called you to do, know that all your hard work is for Him.

4. Don't Make Excuses

Have you ever heard the saying, If it's important to you, you will find a way; if not, you will find an excuse? It's so true, isn't it! We can find every excuse in the world not to do what doesn't come easy. Have you ever said, I don't have the time; I don't have the money; I have a full-time job? These are all possible excuses—excuses to procrastinate!

Think about it. As long as you come up with reasons NOT to look for another job, write a book, take piano lessons, run the marathon, you are setting up roadblocks that can keep you from living your dreams. Take a hard look at what you're really telling yourself. Begin with *new thinking*, and then take action!

Watch carefully what you're doing and how you respond to your self-talk. Watch the lies that you may be feeding yourself. Often the excuse can be, I deserve a break. The famous McDonalds slogan may ring constantly in your mind: "You deserve a break today, so get up and get away...."

Oh, I'm guilty. Night after night I can tell myself, "Take a break, just tonight, just today." And what are your family and friends telling you? I have been told often that everyone needs a break. They mean well. We all need a break from time to time, but in the meantime, could it really mean you're simply procrastinating and making excuses?

Jesus tells a parable of men who were invited to a dinner party and how they made excuses why they were not coming. Luke 14:18 says,

"But they all alike began to make excuses. The first one said to him, 'I have bought a piece of land and I need to go out and look at it; please consider me excused.'" They all made excuses about why they couldn't come, but *really* they just didn't want to go.

Making excuses can be temporary and in time may not be a problem, but it's a *very serious problem* to those who turn away from the Lord and make excuses about *Him*. If you have never studied the book of Romans, I encourage you to do so.

In Romans 1:20-23 we read, "For since the creation of the world His invisible attributes, His eternal power and divine nature, have been clearly seen, being understood through what has been made, so that they are without excuse. For even though they knew God, they did not honor Him as God or give thanks, but they became futile in their speculations, and their foolish heart was darkened. Professing to be wise, they became fools, and exchanged the glory of the incorruptible God for an image in the form of corruptible man and of birds and four-footed animals and crawling creatures."

As I have discussed in other chapters, your relationship with Christ is first and should be supreme over all other areas of your life. But if you have in some way made excuses about God and why you haven't surrendered to Him, consider what these verses are saying.

Know that, in the end, we will have *no excuse*. "So that at the name of Jesus EVERY KNEE WILL BOW, of those who are in heaven and on earth and under the earth, and that every tongue will confess that Jesus Christ is Lord, to the glory of God the Father" (Philippians 2:10-11).

Begin today to stop making excuses and you will see your life dramatically change!

5. Moving Past That Overwhelming Feeling

"According to the American Psychological Association, chronic stress is linked to the six leading causes of death: heart disease, cancer, lung ailments, accidents, cirrhosis of the liver and suicide. And more than 75 percent of all physician office visits are for stress-related ailments and complaints."[25]

Unfortunately, far too many feel overwhelmed and stressed out. It's a serious problem that people in our country face. And for millions, the more stress they feel, the more reason to procrastinate. It's a sad, vicious cycle. It's challenging to set a plan and stick to it. Change requires steady progress, not procrastination.

The process for accomplishing your goals may take a while, but examine why you have that overwhelming feeling to put it off. Often it's due to people working in jobs they don't like, and doing work they are not suited for. This compounds the stress. Have you ever talked to someone who loves their job and heard them say, "Oh, I would do this even if they didn't pay me!"? That's the feeling we all want!

If you constantly feel overwhelmed, consider all that may be causing the stress. Begin to take steps that can help. How's your diet? Do you exercise? These two things alone are vital to helping keep your stress levels down. Ask God to show you the changes that you, personally, can make to relieve your stress and help you toward your life goals.

Everyone will experience stress in their lives at one time or another. And there are seasons of life that bring about more pressures than at other times. There are many helpful things to do, but the number one way to relieve stress is found in Psalm 119:165: "Those who love Your law have great peace, And nothing causes them to stumble." Amazing, isn't it! It's a powerful verse, but it's so true. The person who is passionately seeking God is one who is passionate about His Word, those who love His law! The more you spend time in His Word, the more peace you have. Don't you love that!

As you seek Him, you're given peace, and as you have peace, you will have the will, the "want to," to move toward your goal and change your life!

6. Make the Right Decisions

Wrong decisions may cause pain and could delay your plans for progress toward your dreams. These setbacks can be frustrating, and it's easy to *procrastinate* in order not to mess up again. It can be a form of protection, a hiding place. Over and over the bad decision creates discouraging results; therefore, the disappointment causes you to put off doing anything. Sound familiar?

This is an extremely common problem with procrastination. We want results and we want them now. It's hard to continue when you think you made the wrong choice and you're ready to quit. Don't. Begin again.

God's timing and His direction are key. Our timetable isn't always His. The longer process could be part of God's plan, His training. As you pursue your dreams, pursue His plan in all your decisions. How can you know that you have His direction? First, anything you do that doesn't line up with God's Word cannot be His will. There are clear specific scriptures that give us clear directions.

God tells us to ask Him. James 1:5-8 says, "But if any of you lacks wisdom, let him ask of God, who gives to all generously and without reproach, and it will be given to him. But he must ask in faith without any doubting, for the one who doubts is like the surf of the sea, driven and tossed by the wind. For that man ought not to expect that he will receive anything from the Lord, *being* a double-minded man, unstable in all his ways."

Don't give up. Keep on asking. Daily walk by the Spirit and step out in faith, trusting God to show you what to do next. Think of the outstanding people in our world who had enormous resilience and didn't give up.

Abraham Lincoln was reared in a poor family on the Western Frontier. That didn't stop him from becoming a self-educated lawyer, a Whig party leader, and a state legislator during the late 1830s. He later ran for the United States Senate and lost to his archrival, Democrat Stephen A. Douglas. With this disappointment, it would have been easy to forget politics and move on, but not Lincoln. "In 1860 Lincoln secured the Republican Party presidential nomination as a moderate from a swing state. Though he gained very little support in the slave holding states of the South, Lincoln swept the North and was elected president in 1860."[26] Amazing! Don't you love his story! And, of course, that was just the beginning. Lincoln didn't give up, and he knew how to make the right decisions. He had a passion to make a difference, and he knew his purpose.

7. Know Your Purpose

Have you seen people constantly start new things but never finish them? Over and over they get excited about this new dream, but something happens, and they're now into something completely different. Is this a problem for you? If you know your purpose, you're more likely not to keep procrastinating. Your purpose keeps you going.

It should be no surprise why Rick Warren's book *The Purpose Driven Life* became a New York Times Bestseller with over thirty million copies sold. God created us for a purpose, and He has the perfect plan for our lives. Not having a plan can cause constant procrastination as the search continues.

8. Do You Try to Be Perfect?

Where are you on the list of trying to be perfect? Does this trait help or hinder areas in your life? Certainly it's a great quality for many professions. You don't want your doctors, dentists, and dermatologists to be less than accurate, and you desire for them to be as close to perfect as possible! Right? But as the old saying goes, No one is perfect.

Have you ever thought about the definition of perfectionists? "Perfectionists strain compulsively and unceasingly toward unobtainable goals, and measure their self-worth by productivity and accomplishment. Pressuring oneself to achieve unrealistic goals inevitably sets the person up for disappointment. Perfectionists tend to be harsh critics of themselves when they fail to meet their standards."[27]

Pushing toward high standards can be a wonderful thing; but if you constantly stop and give up on your goals due to perfectionism, this can be a problem. Procrastination can happen as a result of trying to be too perfect.

We are to "in all things show yourself to be an example of good deeds, *with* purity in doctrine, dignified, sound *in* speech which is beyond reproach, so that the opponent will be put to shame, having nothing bad to say about us" (Titus 2:7-8).

It's our lifestyle, our pursuit of righteousness, that God is most concerned about, not perfectionism. We know that whatever we do in word or deed, we are to do all in the name of the Lord Jesus Christ (Colossians 3:17).

Don't let being less than perfect keep you from earnestly reaching your goals. Enjoy your journey without being so hard on yourself!

9. Are You Motivated?

As I have studied and observed many people who have impacted our world, I've found a common thread in countless lives: their pursuit to make a difference can often come out of the pain they've experienced in their own lives.

This isn't always true with those who are motivated by pleasure. You can see this from some of the famous music celebrities as they begin to trash their lives after they lose focus and purpose. Often they may end up with too much free time and with an exorbitant amount of money. Their pursuit of pleasure often takes them to jail, to drug rehab centers, or to bankruptcy. Don't you find that interesting? They lost their motivation, and their idle time led them to trouble. This doesn't stop the tabloids from talking about them. It gives them more news to share about their sad existence. And it *is* sad. We know from the book of Ecclesiastes that King Solomon had it all and it wasn't enough.

I said to myself, "Come now, I will test you with pleasure. So enjoy yourself." And behold, it too was futility.
—**Ecclesiastes 2:1**

What is motivating you? When you're motivated enough, you stop procrastinating. Are you letting your hurts and heartbreaks stop you, or could you be motivated by them? It's a choice!

When I think of someone who could have slipped into self-pity, I think of Mary Kay Ash. Mary Kay did not have it easy. Ash was married at age seventeen, had three children, and her husband served in World War II. Mary Kay sold books door-to-door. After her husband's return in 1945, they divorced.

"Ash went to work for Stanley Home Products. Frustrated when passed over for a promotion in favor of a man that she had trained, Ash retired in 1963 and intended to write a book to assist women in business. The book turned into a business plan for her ideal company, and in the summer of 1963, Mary Kay and her new husband, Mel Ash, planned to start Mary Kay Cosmetics. However, one month before Mary Kay and Mel Ash started Beauty by Mary Kay, as the company was then called, Mel died of a heart attack. One month after Mel's death on September 13, 1963, when she was 45 years old with a $5,000 investment from her oldest son, Ben Rogers, Jr. and with her young son, Richard Rogers taking her late husband's place, Ash started Mary Kay Cosmetics. The company started its original storefront operation in Dallas."[28]

What an amazing story! Today, "Mary Kay, Inc. is an American privately owned multi-level marketing direct sales company that sells cosmetic products. According to Direct Selling News, Mary Kay was the sixth largest direct selling company in the world in 2011, with net sales of USD 2.9 billion."[29] "A long-time fundraiser for charities, she founded the Mary Kay Ash Charitable Foundation to raise money to combat domestic violence and cancers affecting women."[30] Mary Kay Ash was motivated and she didn't let her painful past hinder her from doing what she felt called to do.

What is holding you back? What is causing you to procrastinate? No matter what has happened in your life, God has you in the palm of His hand, and He has a plan!

Our greatest fear should not be of failure, but of succeeding at something that doesn't really matter.

—D.L. Moody

Step Seven: Move Again

1. Consider why you procrastinate.

2. Make a list of the things that you put off doing and record why you're delaying working toward these things.

3. Does disappointment continue to set you back?

4. Every time you know you're procrastinating, try to stop and do something that's positive. Watch carefully how you're spending your time.

5. Daily, prayerfully seek the Lord for clear direction.

6. Stop delaying and move again!!

Prayer: Dear Lord, I confess that at times I can really be lazy. It is my desire to make changes. Help me to see when I am procrastinating and when I truly need the time to rest. I know that in my strength I can do nothing. It's only in Your power that I can accomplish much. Take my life and use it for Your glory. The tasks ahead may be great; help me not to be overwhelmed with the journey. You are the reason for all that I do. To You be the glory. Amen.

Chapter 8

Aim High

Plan Again

Success is not measured by the things you do compared to what others do. It is measured by what you do with the ability God gave you.

—Zig Ziglar

Somewhere Over the Rainbow" was sung by Judy Garland in the movie *The Wizard of Oz* in 1939, and it continues to be a classic beloved song. There is something very special about that song.

The moving melody along with its lyrics stirs your heart. So what is it that makes this song so special? The powerful line that I believe captures the hearts of so many is "And the dreams that you dare to dream really do come true."

People desperately want their dreams to come true. What about you? Are your dreams coming true, or is there an ache in your heart because you feel like your dreams are never going to happen?

Continue to aim high, dream big, BUT have a plan. Many miss the mark because they didn't have a mark. You must have a target to hit a bull's eye. Do you have any kind of plan, or could it be you've simply lost your focus? Good question!

Merriam-Webster defines the word *focus*, (verb): "to cause (something, such as attention) to be directed at something specific; to direct your attention or effort at something specific; to adjust (something, such as lens or a camera) to make an image clear."[31] Do you have a clear purpose, a clear calling on where you are going? What has your attention? This is so important to ever reaching your God-given dreams. You must stay close to Him to know what He is calling you to do.

Proverbs 4:25-27 says, "Let your eyes look directly ahead And let your *gaze* be *fixed* straight in front of you. Watch the path of your feet And all your ways will be established. Do not turn to the right nor to the left; Turn your foot from evil." (Italics added.)

I love these verses! Do you want all your ways to be established by Him? It's amazing that this is even possible, *but it is*! These simple but profound words from the Book of Proverbs are not always easy to live, but it is critically important that you're living a life fully devoted to God.

To hear God's voice and to discern His will and direction, you must be still and listen. You must be seeking Him, looking for Him, and listening for Him. It takes intentional, concentrated effort! It's tuning out all around you, focusing on Him, and digging deep into His Word. Do you do this? Do you try to hear from Him? Do you take the moments of quietness and solitude to hear Him speak? Daily begin taking the first steps. Begin stepping out and moving forward one step at a time.

The often overused quote "Rome wasn't built in a day" is so true. The magnificent city was built with a plan and with a purpose. Great accomplishments often come from those with intense, fixed focus! Michelangelo certainly had remarkable focus. "As a child, Michelangelo told his father, 'Deprive me of art and there will not be enough liquid in me to spit.' Michelangelo became one of the greatest artists of all time because he knew how to focus with a passion on what was important to him. A person's ability to focus is like a magnifying glass that directs the rays of the sun with such intensity that they can ignite paper or burn into wood."[32] Amazing!

It's certainly not always easy to have exceptional focus. We live in a busy world that's constantly filling our minds with noise! It's difficult even to think clearly at times, much less discern and hear God's voice. Everybody and everything has our attention. Now, with all the social media platforms, it's easy to be drawn in; and before you know it, an hour has passed. I know this all too well. I go to Facebook and think I will look for just a minute, but it becomes much longer! Can you relate?

Focus—plan, prepare! If you feel like God has called you to write a book, get started! Has He called you to go on a mission trip, to dedicate more time at your church, to change careers, to birth a ministry for teens, or to build a soup kitchen? Whatever it is, it will take time, energy, and a very clear plan.

> Therefore be careful how you walk, not as unwise men but as wise, making the most of your time, because the days are evil.
> **—Ephesians 5:15-16**

We're living in perilous days. The days are evil, days like we have never seen before. The way we spend our time is critical.

In 2 Timothy 3:1-5 we see this:

But realize this, that in the last days difficult times will come. For men will be lovers of self, lovers of money, boastful, arrogant, revilers, disobedient to parents, ungrateful, unholy, unloving, irreconcilable, malicious gossips, without self-control, brutal, haters of good, treacherous, reckless, conceited, lovers of pleasure rather than lovers of God, holding to a form of godliness, although they have denied its power; Avoid such men as these.

Does this sound like our world today? Time is short, make the most of it! Press through whatever is holding you back and move toward what God may be calling you to. "Just do it," as Nike says. How do you get there? You get there with prayer, Bible study, a support team, and clearly defined goals.

Pray, pray, pray! Satan would like nothing more than have you head in the wrong direction, spend time in an area you're not gifted in, and end up in frustration. So pray.

Over and over we see Jesus getting away to pray. "After He had sent the crowds away, He went up on the mountain by Himself to pray; and when it was evening, He was there alone" (Matthew 14:23). Do whatever it takes to get alone and pray.

Build a winning team around you. Your cheerleading squad (as I call them) is *very important* to accomplishing your God-given dreams and goals. First, godly friends should tell you the truth. My spiritual team that surrounds me lets me know if I'm headed in the wrong direction. I ask them to be brutally honest with me. You should have a Dream Team that will do the same with you. Your team should be made up of godly people who will encourage, support, and help push you toward your God-given dreams and goals. Keep in mind, there will always be the *negative nannies*, as I call them. They are the ones who see the glass as half-empty, not half-full. Listen to them, consider what they say, but don't let them discourage you from keeping on. Just be aware. When I was working on my first book, I had another author tell me how hard it was to be published and that maybe I should just write articles. They were right; it is hard; but had I listened and only done that, I may not have ever been published. Be very careful whom you listen to.

1. Keep praying.
2. Keep seeking the Lord through Bible study.
3. Continue to seek godly counsel.

When God begins birthing His plan in your heart and your Dream Team supports the direction you are headed, *make a plan*. A plan should be easy, not difficult. I have read many books on goals and meeting deadlines with charts, graphs, papers, and planners. All that can be good, and that might work for you. I need *simplicity*—something I can handle and easily follow. I believe in keeping it simple!

Let's use a word that is easy to remember—DREAM. If you follow my DREAM PLAN, watch out! You may be unstoppable! Start today with your own

DREAM PLAN

Decide what your dreams and goals are. This is the problem with so many; they don't make goals or have plans. Decide where you're going, and God will help take you there if it's His will and plan for your life.

Determine that you will do something every day that will help move you toward your dream. This is vitally important! Every single day do something toward your goal. Baby steps grow into larger steps. There will be a day when you'll run toward your goal because you can see the finish line! You've heard the old adage, How do you eat an elephant? One bite at a time. It's true! Daily take steps to take you closer to your dream.

Dedication that's unstoppable. You will have disappointments along the way. I know of no one who breezed through God-given dreams without some setbacks. The enemy doesn't want you to thrive. He desires for you to live in a survival mode, to live a life without dreams, a life that we dread, a life without purpose. Be dedicated to live a life that only God can do through you.

Remember why you're working toward your goal. You may be working two jobs and going to school. You're overwhelmed. Remember, it won't always be this way. Keep taking it one day at a time.

Read something every day that increases your knowledge toward your God-given dream. Today you can instantly find a blog or book on the Internet. The world is at your fingertips. You have no excuses. Reading helps you keep learning and growing so that one day you can be an expert in your field.

Rely on God. "'I am the vine, you are the branches; he who abides in Me and I in him, he bears much fruit, for apart from Me you can do nothing'" (John 15:5). Your goal should be to bear much fruit. Stay close to Him, and rely on Him.

Enjoy the journey! I must admit, this one is a hard one for me. Our ultimate joy is in the Lord, not in the blessings or the dreams. "You will make known to me the path of life; In Your presence is fullness of joy; In Your right hand there are pleasures forever" (Psalm 16:11). Today is all we have; in all our pursuits, our ultimate passion should be time with our Father. We are *alive* in Christ. He gives us our joy—don't forget this on the journey.

Evaluate where you are. Look at your plans, your goals, and see how you're doing. Do you need to pick up your pace a little? If are you about to give up, don't! If you need to adjust how you're spending your time, do so.

Aim high! God desires for you to be your best. Far too many are aiming low, thinking they're not good enough, smart enough, and talented enough for their dreams. But Psalm 139:13 says, "For You formed my inward parts; You wove me in my mother's womb." Be the person God created you to be!

Appreciate those around you. If your Dream Team is supportive and helpful to you, thank them often. Go to lunch, have them over for dinner, do something to show them how much you appreciate them. Their prayers and godly support are critical in this process.

Applaud your successes. Along your journey it's important to see how far you have come. It's important that you don't beat yourself up! It's easy to want to be at the finish line, but great goals typically take time. Ouch! I don't like it either, but applaud your successes in the process! If you're just starting, that's wonderful! Applaud yourself, you're on your way!

Map out where you are going. Plans are necessary. Make a simple strategy for how you will accomplish your goals. Keep it simple, but make it effective. Make a list of your plans, and put this map on your bathroom mirrors and on your refrigerator. Determine dates and deadlines for steps along your journey. Deadlines are vital to ever finishing your goal.

Motivation from others is priceless! Who motivates you? Do you have influencers in your life that encourage you and help push you toward your dreams? Zig Ziglar has always been one that motivates me. If I need a push, I simply google Zig and find his many videos and articles. His life was dedicated to pointing others toward their God-given dreams no matter their obstacles.

Move toward your goal. It's important that you keep moving! Continual movement toward your dreams helps you keep going. Daily you will see progress, and you will begin to see your goals unfolding. It gets exciting! Movement is necessary! Don't stop.

What's keeping you from moving ahead? Do negative thoughts plague you? Have you been told that nothing good will ever happen to you? Have past experiences and critical words from someone stopped you from stepping out and taking a risk?

Dr. Howard Hendricks, a former professor at Dallas Theological Seminary, chose to listen to the positive encouragement of an elementary school teacher rather than all the negative things that surrounded him in his adolescent years.

"Howard Hendricks was raised in a broken home. He recalled, 'My parents separated when I came along. I split the family.' His father's mother reared him, and he described himself as a 'troublemaker' during his elementary school years, 'probably just "acting out" a lot of insecurities.'

"'Most likely to end up in prison' was the assessment of his fifth-grade teacher in Philadelphia. Once she even tied him to his seat with a rope and taped his mouth shut. Yet everything changed for that boy when he met his sixth-grade teacher. He introduced himself to Miss Noe, and she told him, 'I've heard a lot about you. But I don't believe a word of it.'

"Those words would change his life. She made him realize for the first time that someone cared. 'People are always looking for someone to say, "Hey, I believe in you,"' he said. And in his more than sixty years as a professor, he believed in his students."[33]

I love Dr. Hendricks's story. Imagine how different his life might have been if he had chosen to embrace the harsh lies told to him by Miss Simons! But, thank God for Miss Noe; she clearly understood the power of helpful and heartfelt words that build others up, rather than words that tear people down.

God wants you to believe Him no matter what has happened in your past. Is there anything standing in your way of making plans for God-sized dreams?

When you dare to do great things, then keep going and never give up. Courage believes that it's never too late to dream, it's never too late to accomplish our goals. If you are following God's plan for your life and you believe you will win, then chances are you will.

Martin Luther King, Jr. said, "Faith is taking the first step, even when you don't see the whole staircase."[34] God wants us to dare to believe Him again, and again, and again. Make a plan, follow your plan, and begin walking toward your God-given dreams. Never stop pushing forward, aiming high, and dreaming big!

"…if you have faith the size of a mustard seed, you will say to this mountain, 'Move from here to there,' and it will move; and nothing will be impossible to you."
—Matthew 17:20

Don't you love that!

Step Eight: Plan Again

1. What is keeping you from making a plan?

2. Start this week by praying and seeking God about His divine plan for your life.

3. Begin writing down your DREAM PLANS.

4. Put your DREAM PLAN in three prominent places where you will see it, possibly on your smart phone, refrigerator, and mirror.

5. Do something every day toward your plan.

6. Plan again and don't lose heart.

Prayer: Lord, I give You all my plans and dreams. Help me to stay focused and do what You have called me to do. May I not lose heart; as disappointments come, help me to keep going and to take the next step. Also help me to enjoy the journey. I know with You, God, "'All things are possible'" (Mark 10:27). Thank You for Your great love and mercy. Amen.

Chapter 9

Tired of Waiting?

Wait Again

It's never too late to be what you might have been.
—George Eliot

as your dream been dashed one more time? You've stepped out in faith believing now is the time to move and nothing seems to be going right. Does it mean you didn't hear correctly from God and maybe you've gone in the wrong direction?

I don't know your situation, but I do know that God's timing and plans are often not the same as ours.

Do you like to wait? Most don't and I don't. Yet in the pursuit of our goals, often there are interruptions, set-backs, and disappointments.

When things happen, finances become difficult, and you're ready to forget your dreams because the waiting is getting too hard, wait again! Wait some more and never give up!

Waiting can be as simple as waiting in line at the grocery store, waiting for your food to cook, or waiting at the doctor's office. I recently visited a new cardiologist. My eye doctor had requested that I see a heart doctor due to my very low blood pressure and erratic heartbeat.

I knew this might be somewhat of a wait since I was a new patient, *but* I waited and waited and waited some more. I finally asked a lady at the front desk if I could just step outside for a minute. I walked up and down the sidewalk, trying to get a little exercise. It was a beautiful day, and I began to think of all the wonderful things I could be doing instead of waiting in a cold dark room at a doctor's office.

Before I saw the doctor, every patient and every person was gone from the waiting room. Oh yes, it was a waiting room alright, and I was the very last one to be called! I finally heard, "Ms. Hardaway," and I jumped up and almost ran to the door! I had waited for over two hours. The good news, after finally seeing the doctor—there were no problems with my heart!

I still wanted to get upset because of the wait. I knew I had arrived earlier than other patients, and yet, I was called last. No one who worked in the office seemed to really care. I didn't understand how a two-hour wait was not a big deal. Most simply say, "You're at the doctor's office and that's normal."

Waiting is normal, but it can be hard and very inconvenient. In most all cases, and especially in the pursuit of major changes in your life, the wait is challenging. So how do you keep on waiting? Are you in a waiting room instead of being where you would like it to be?

During these waiting periods, you may not understand why those around you don't seem sympathetic to the long and possibly tumultuous time you have had while pursuing your dreams and your goals. But very often it's necessary to wait. It's not only necessary, but it may be God's very best plan for you.

When your goals overtake the peace and contentment in your life, it's possible you're not resting in where God has you. It isn't easy because the tug in your heart in the pursuit of your dream is real. It may be that your dream is God's direction for your life. *But* in your journey, in the pursuit, could it be that there are still some wonderful opportunities and hidden jewels right where you are today?

"Years ago, Russell Conwell told of an ancient Persian, Ali Hafed, who 'owned a very large farm that had orchards, grain fields, and gardens…and was a wealthy contented man.' One day a wise man from the East told the farmer all about diamonds and how wealthy he would be if he owned a diamond mine. Ali Hafed went to bed that night a poor man—poor because he was discontented. Craving a mine of diamonds, he sold his farm to search for the rare stones. He traveled the world over, finally becoming so poor, broken, and defeated that he committed suicide. One day the man who purchased Ali Hafed's farm led his camel into the garden to drink. As his camel put its nose into the brook, the man saw a flash of light from the sands of the stream. He pulled out a stone that reflected all the hues of the rainbow. The man had discovered the diamond mine of Golcanda, the most magnificent mine in all of history. Had Ali Hafed remained at home, and dug in his own garden, then instead of death in a strange land, he would have had acres of diamonds."[35]

Oh my friend, don't miss the diamonds that may be in your present job, with your family, in your church, and in your own community. The grass may not be greener on the other side.

For now, would you look for the possible diamonds that you may already have? Find something good in your present situation and dwell on the good things. There may not be many, but ask God to show you what you might be missing. In your journey today, be the very best you can be right where you are.

Live each day with passion! We don't know what will happen tomorrow or the next day or in the months and years to come. In your journey look for the jewels in your own yard—the place you are right now. What diamonds are you possibly missing this very day?

Have you ever thought about how diamonds are made? Most natural diamonds are made over a very, very long time and require incredibly intense heat and enormous pressure.

Is that how you feel? You're under intense pressure—pressure you don't like. God may be allowing this season in your life for a very specific purpose: a season of refining your character. It's not fun and certainly may not at all seem fair. God is molding and shaping you into His image if you let Him.

Life is not fair. It's not fair possibly in your work place, your home situation, or your financial situation. Before anyone even heard of identity theft, a friend of mine and her husband had all the money they had in the bank stolen from them through identify fraud. They have never recovered their money, but that hasn't stopped my friend from continuing her ministry of writing books, speaking, and having a counseling center. She persevered through a painful, horrendous time. She chose to view her circumstance as an opportunity to show the world Who was in charge of her life. She trusted God in it all.

This is what we all must do: trust God. We must trust God when He appears to be silent in trying situations. When life's difficulties come, what do you do? People numb their pain in countless ways. I've watched many try to drown out their pain with music. They're constantly wearing a headset with music pounding in their ears while their heart is still hurting. Where do you run?

King David often ran to God and cried out to Him in times of distress, and he waited for the Lord. You see this in many of his writings in the Psalms.

I waited patiently for the LORD;
And He inclined to me and heard my cry.
He brought me up out of the pit of destruction, out of the miry clay,
And He set my feet upon a rock making my footsteps firm.
He put a new song in my mouth, a song of praise to our God;
Many will see and fear
And will trust in the LORD.

How blessed is the man who has made the LORD his trust,
And has not turned to the proud, nor to those who lapse into falsehood.
Many, O LORD my God, are the wonders which You have done,
And Your thoughts toward us;
There is none to compare with You.
If I would declare and speak of them,
They would be too numerous to count.
—Psalm 40:1-5

There are so many rich truths just in these few verses. First, you see David *waiting patiently for the LORD*. He ran to God, knowing He would bring comfort and hope. Over and over you see David running to God and waiting.

Don't try waiting in your own strength. David was eager to hear from the Lord. As David spent time with Him, he moved from his distress to security. He sang praises. David said that God "put a new song in his mouth." What a contrast!

Over and over throughout Scripture acts of praise is a common theme. So in your problems, praise Him. In your waiting, praise Him. In your times of distress, praise Him. You wait and you praise. Life can have many unexpected twists and turns, and yet you never know what may be right around the corner. Don't simply wait and fume or wait and worry! Sing praises!

Waiting *is* hard, especially when today you see many entrepreneurs have been wildly successful at a young age. Yet that is certainly not always the norm. Ray Kroc said, "I was an overnight success alright, but 30 years is a long, long night."[36] He was referring, of course, to his life prior to becoming a success story. His life journey started young.

"In 1917, 15-year-old Ray Kroc lied about his age to join the Red Cross as an ambulance driver, but the war ended before he completed his training. He then worked as a piano player, a paper cup salesman and a Multi-mixer salesman.

"In 1954, he visited a restaurant in San Bernardino, California that had purchased several Multi-mixers. There he found a small but successful restaurant run by brothers Dick and Mac McDonald, and was stunned by the effectiveness of their operation. They produced a limited menu, concentrating on just a few items—burgers, fries and beverages—which allowed them to focus on quality and quick service.

"Kroc pitched his vision of creating McDonald's restaurants all over the U.S. to the brothers. In 1955, he founded McDonald's System, Inc., a predecessor of the McDonald's Corporation, and six years later bought the exclusive rights to the McDonald's name. By 1958, McDonald's had sold its 100 millionth hamburger."[37]

It was later in life that Ray Kroc found his unique skills as a businessman and became a brilliant innovator in the fast food business.

If you're in a season of waiting, try not to get discouraged. Keep in mind, there are amazing people who had great accomplishments later in life. As a young girl, I watched the popular television series *Little House on the Prairie*. At the time it didn't occur to me where these programs originated.

Laura Ingalls Wilder, author of *Little House on the Prairie*, has written some of the world's most beloved children's books. "Wilder's first novel was not published until she was 65 years old. She later wrote 12 more books in her series."[38] It's amazing to think that long past Laura's life, her books continue to be published and give joy to many throughout the world.

Don't lose your dream. Don't lose your zeal to push forward. Waiting can be challenging and difficult, but wait some more.

Our modern-day technologies have helped provide and enhance our abilities to have so much instantly. The smartphone is amazingly smart alright. Just ask Siri; she will tell you most anything. To find information on a subject, you used to have to take time to go to a library, look in a filing cabinet drawer, find a book or encyclopedia, and then begin researching to find the information you needed. Now, thanks to modern technology, we can get any information almost instantly.

We know from Ecclesiastes 3:1 that "There is an appointed time for everything. And there is a time for every event under heaven." Often the great men of God were mightily used much later in their lives. God molded and shaped their character for the enormous tasks He would later give to them.

I ask you again, have you truly stopped and taken an overview of your life? Have you looked for milestones that have happened in your life? Have you looked for answered prayers and ways you know God has moved and worked in your life along the way? It's helpful to do this.

Let's take an aerial view of Moses' life, an amazing life to observe! God worked in three distinct forty-year periods.

For forty years Moses lives as a Prince in Egypt, but things dramatically changed. Moses killed an Egyptian slave master. In

Exodus 2:14 we see, "'...Are you intending to kill me as you did the Egyptian?'...." Moses realizes that his criminal act is known and he knows he must flee.

He moves to Midian and there he stays in the wilderness for forty years. His life moves from a Prince in Egypt to a shepherd living in the desert. What a contrast! Imagine the change, the humility, the enormously different kind of life this was. Oh, but God was in every detail! God was working humility into Moses' life as he became a husband, a father, and a shepherd. God was busy teaching Moses how to live life in a dessert, in a wilderness. He prepared him for each calling.

Have you considered what God might be teaching you, what He wants to teach you? God doesn't waste anything. He's molding and preparing you just like he did with Moses. God was building Moses' character to take on one of the greatest challenges in human history. After forty years in the wilderness, Moses heard God's holy call.

Think of the enormous challenge, the enormous calling, and the enormous character that God had worked in Moses' life. He was chosen to be the man who would move 600,000 Hebrew slaves out of Egypt (Exodus 12:37).

Moses was eighty years old when his call came. This calling, this move, this task changed the course of history.

> "Therefore, come now, and I will send you to Pharaoh, so that you may bring My people, the sons of Israel, out of Egypt." But Moses said to God, "Who am I, that I should go to Pharaoh, and that I should bring the sons of Israel out of Egypt?" And He said, "Certainly I will be with you, and this shall be the sign to you that it is I who have sent you: when you have brought the people out of Egypt, you shall worship God at this mountain."
>
> **—Exodus 3:10-12**

There was no way Moses could do this enormous task in his own strength. We learn more about Moses' call from Exodus 3:13-14, 15b.

Then Moses said to God, "Behold, I am going to the sons of Israel, and I will say to them, 'The God of your fathers has sent me to you.' Now they may say to me, 'What is His name?' What shall I say to them?" God said to Moses, "I AM WHO I AM"; and He said, "Thus you shall say to the sons of Israel, 'I AM has sent me to you.'" God, furthermore, said to Moses, "Thus you shall say to the sons of Israel, 'The Lord, the God of your fathers, the God of Abraham, the God of Isaac, and the God of Jacob, has sent me to you.'"

"This is My name forever, and this is My memorial-name to all generations."

Oh my friend, be patient, persevere, and push ahead. God is working when you just may not see it. Your calling must be in God's timing and when you go, go in God's strength and in His power. The great I AM is with you also.

God can do the miraculous, the unbelievable miracles in your life as well. As I consider our godly leaders today, many are doing some of their best and most remarkable work in their eighties. It's a fantastic example of perseverance, purpose, and calling on their lives. There is no retirement for those who are passionate about being used by God until their home-going.

Whether you're waiting for a different job, waiting to be married, waiting to have children, or waiting for the success you've worked for—trust God.

Don't lose heart and don't give up! I love the story of Anna Mary Robertson, better known as Grandma Moses. She is "one of the biggest names in American folk art, and she didn't even pick up a brush until she was well into her eighth decade. Grandma Moses was originally a big fan of embroidery, but once her arthritis grew too painful for her to hold a needle, she decided to give painting a try in the mid-1930s. She was 76 when she cranked out her first canvas, and she lived another 25 years as a painter—long enough to see the canvases she had sold for $3 fetch prices north of $10,000.00."[39] This is an amazing story of a woman who had a passion for the arts.

What is your passion? Your God-given gifts will always burn within you, and I encourage you to never let them die. No one else is gifted just like you are. No one else has the exact same calling God has placed on your life. And no one else can do what you're to do.

In the waiting, keep praying, waiting expectantly, and praising God. Don't lose heart and don't lose hope. Suddenly, when you don't expect it, God breaks through!

When it looks like nothing is happening in your life and you're just not sure what to do, hold on! You may be like the butterfly in the *chrysalis* time in your life!

Have you ever spent much time thinking about how a butterfly is formed? It's quite amazing; simple, yet profound. The lifecycle of a butterfly begins with eggs; changes to caterpillar (larva), to chrysalis (pupa), then to a butterfly (adult, imago).

The chrysalis is the critical time for the butterfly. "A chrysalis…or nympha is the pupal stage of butterflies…. When the caterpillar is fully grown, it makes a button of silk which it uses to fasten its body to a leaf or a twig. Then the caterpillar's skin comes off for the final time. Under this old skin is a hard skin called a chrysalis."[40]

In the chrysalis time of your life, God does His glorious work, and the transformation is happening. Think of it. When you feel frail, hopeless, wondering when your life is ever going to change, you may be soon getting ready to fly!

God is forming, working, and changing you; let Him do His work. Get ready, get excited, get ready for the flight of your life! He wants you to soar! Remember, in your patience, keep pursuing God first and watch what happens.

> Yet those who wait for the LORD
> Will gain new strength;
> They will mount up *with* wings like eagles,
> They will run and not get tired,
> They will walk and not become weary.
> **—Isaiah 40:31**

Step Nine: Wait Again

1. Are you ready to give up because you're tired of waiting? Realize that is what the enemy would like you to do. *Never give up.*

2. Remember what God did in the life of Moses. He had three forty-year periods that God remarkably used to change all of history. God is molding and shaping you during these days of waiting. *Keep pressing on.*

3. It's never too late to pursue your dreams. Remember Laura Ingalls Wilder? Her work still lives on today. Your work may live way past your life. It's a remarkable thing that God can do through your life.

4. If you're tired of waiting, do something productive to keep on going. It's never too late.

5. Stay in touch with your DREAM Team. Pray and purpose to keep going. Don't stop praying every single day. Give God all the glory daily.

Prayer: Dear Lord, I'm tired. I'm tired of the waiting and the not knowing what is going to happen next. I'm tired of the difficult circumstances that seem to continue in my life. Help me to trust you when the challenges remain painful. God, help my unbelief. Help me to stand in the waiting room as long as I need to be there. Help me to move when it's time, and I praise you in the desert and dry time I find myself in. You are the great I AM, and I cling to your Word that tells me you have a plan and a purpose. Help me to believe again.

Chapter 10

Only Thirty Days

Live Again

A ship is safe in harbor, but that is not what ships are for.
—William Shedd

I received a text from my cousin that said, "It appears a tornado is headed your way and people are being encouraged to take shelter." That evening I was visiting with my mother and immediately we started making our way to her safe room. This room was built for strong storms, and we hoped and prayed we didn't have to see just how safe it really was.

While sitting in a small cement block room, we only had a cell phone, a blanket, a chair, a commode, and pillows. While I was constantly looking at my iPhone to see what I could find out about the weather, I also had time to briefly think about my life and what really was important. Mom and I began praying for safety and for God's protection.

During challenging times like this, no money, no person, nothing can help if you can't leave your shelter. Nothing could really keep us safe but God. And there will be a day for everyone when no amount of financial security, family, or friends can help. If a doctor's report determines that you only have one month or so to live, everything changes, doesn't it? Life is fragile.

Thank God, the tornado did not strike downtown Nashville that evening and we were safe; however, in many parts of the region, others did get hit. It's sad, it's sobering, and it's very real that we truly have no idea how long we'll live.

If you knew you had only thirty days left, how would you live? Suddenly the size of your house and the make and model of your car doesn't really matter. Your relationships become front and center; all your worldly positions are unimportant.

Your estate and material things will be distributed, depending on your will. Some things will be sold to strangers, and in time, your money will be spent by others. It's a hard reality but true; everyone will someday stop breathing. After you spend your entire life acquiring things, in an instant they'll be gone from you. And as the saying goes, You can't take it with you. We know this, but do we really embrace the reality of it?

I urge you to make a list of things you would do, or do differently, if you had only thirty days left. As you do this, your attitude toward your work, your church, your family, and your friends may truly change. Your relationships with family, friends, and with God are critical, no matter your health or financial status. Good relationships are biblical and basic to living life in peace.

All the dreams, goals, and plans should take back seat to getting your relationships right. You may get on a fast track of a new career and continue to avoid the critically important areas in your life: your family and friends. Is there someone who has deeply wounded you, said things that you've never forgotten? Has anyone done things that have caused you such pain that you've moved on and you've tried to bury the hurt? However, you know it's there, and you try to avoid the person who hurt you. Begin today to prayerfully consider how you can forgive them if you haven't. If your situation needs addressing and you need to personally talk through the event, the hurt, then seek God's wisdom as to how you should contact and talk to them.

We see in the gospel of Mark just how important forgiveness is: "'Whenever you stand praying, forgive, if you have anything against anyone, so that your Father who is in heaven will also forgive you your transgressions. But if you do not forgive, neither will your Father who is in heaven forgive your transgressions'" (Mark 11:25-26). This is a serious matter to God. Often the tendency is to stuff it, shake it off, or just ignore that the problem exists.

Maybe you've tried to forgive and you are tired of forgiving. I understand; but as you continue to ignore the situation, the bitterness will build. Have you wondered, How long do I keep forgiving? Peter the apostle asked the same thing: "Then Peter came and said to Him, 'Lord, how often shall my brother sin against me and I forgive him? Up to seven times?' Jesus said to him, 'I do not say to you, up to seven times, but up to seventy times seven'" (Matthew 18:21-22).

You forgive and forgive and, when you're tired of forgiving, you forgive again. This is impossible in your own strength and in your own power. But through the Holy Spirit working in and through you, you can walk in forgiveness as much and as often as you need to. Jesus never tells us to do anything that is not possible. We know that with God all things are possible (Matthew 19:26). As you seek a new place in your life, forgiveness is truly the place to start.

If you're feeling powerless, keep praying; keep seeking the Lord to help you walk through the difficulties in relationships. When someone has harsh words, it's easy to lash back in the same tone. "Be kind to one another, tender-hearted, forgiving each other, just as God in Christ also has forgiven you" (Ephesians 4:32).

Not only are we to forgive, but on top of that, we're to be kind. In the stresses and challenges that relationships have, kindness is a must. I have blown it in this area at times, and I would assume most have, but we just start over and begin again. Last night was a dreadful rainy night, but today is a sunny beautiful day. Each new day brings a different set of circumstances and a whole host of new things where you can begin again. Life can look very different each and every new day. Start again! It's a brand spanking new day!

If you knew you only had a short time to live, you probably would begin examining the potential areas in your life that you would like to change and you just might begin taking more risks. It's interesting that the term *bucket list* has become such a popular phrase! Often when I talk with people about their dreams, they tell me a list of things they desire to do and many say, "It's on my bucket list!"

The list can often look like this: travel more, run a marathon, cross America in an RV, spend more time with family, write a book, go back to school, jump out of an airplane, and get in shape. When time seems to be short, people risk more and plan more, because if they don't, they believe they'll never do any of these things.

This bucket list describes some of things I would like to do. The jumping out of an airplane is still up in the air. But, as I look over the list, the real urgency for me would be to finish this book! My heart truly is to make an impact on God's kingdom. And in the end, that should be your heart's desire as well.

I will never forget the day I heard Rick Warren share his story about his dad's last words to him.

"The night before my father died, my wife, my niece, and I were in his bedroom by his side. Dad suddenly became very agitated and tried to get out of bed," Warren continued. "Of course, he was too weak to get up so Kay insisted he lay back down. But he kept persisting in trying to get out of bed. Finally, Kay in exasperation said 'Jimmy, you CANNOT get up! You are dying. We will get you whatever you need. What are you trying to do?'

"My dad replied, 'I've got to save one more for Jesus! I've got to save one more for Jesus! One more for Jesus! One more for Jesus!' He began to repeat that phrase over and over and over. It is no exaggeration to say that during the next hour, he repeated the phrase probably a hundred times: 'Got to save one more for Jesus!'"

Warren said that as he sat by his bed with tears flowing down his cheeks, he bowed his head to thank God for the legacy of his father's compassionate faith.

"While my head was bowed, my dad reached out and placed his frail hand on my head and said, as if commissioning me with a sacred calling, 'Reach one more for Jesus! Reach one more for Jesus!' It was a holy moment and I knew what I was supposed to do the rest of my life, regardless of problems, illnesses, conflicts, critics, attacks, delays, difficulties, or any other barriers."...[41]

Rick's dad said, simply and clearly, what we're supposed to do. It's not complicated, it's not difficult, it's not hard. As Christians our life ambition should be to "Reach one more for Jesus."

God's calling on our lives comes to each of us in a wide variety of ways, but in the end, our ultimate goal should be impacting more lives for God's Kingdom. In this book we've discussed life's challenges, setbacks, opportunities, goals, and gifting. What are you doing with what God has given to you today?

Far too many look at life in two ways: looking backwards thinking about the good old days or looking forward to the future. Learning from the past can be a good thing, and pushing toward your dream goals is a great thing. But today, begin enjoying the journey more by being grateful right where you are. It's not easy, so consider the thirty-day challenge to begin living again. As the frustrations of life continue to flood your day, think about how you would respond if you knew you only had a short time left.

Having a life that is full of gratitude is vastly important. Every single thing you have is a gift from the Lord. We know this from James 1:17, "Every good thing given and every perfect gift is from above, coming down from the Father of lights, with whom there is no variation or shifting shadow." If you believe this, do you continue to complain? Having a negative attitude can become a habit and can influence your thinking and the thinking of those you are around.

Do you consider yourself a grateful person or one who is always expecting more? Are you worn out with the media constantly telling you that the more you have the happier you'll be? I'll never forget a television program I was watching about the rich and famous. One of the many outrageous things being done was with a group of people at a party enjoying pouring bottles of champagne (each bottle was worth thousands) on each other. It was opulence in its worst form.

Many are aspiring to become multi-millionaires and billionaires. Certainly God has gifted people to do this, but what is really important is how they will impact eternity. How they will spend their time and talents is what matters.

When you think of the Fortune 500 companies and the list of entrepreneurs who started these companies, one name probably comes to mind: Steve Jobs. Many have a strong interest in Job's life because Apple's products have greatly changed the way we live. Don't you think it's interesting that the products begin with the letter *i*?

It's hard to imagine our world without iTunes, iPods, iPhones, and iPads. Yet, the founder is gone. Jobs lived from February 24, 1955 to October 5, 2011 and died of pancreatic cancer at the age of fifty-six. It's sad to think about how his life ended.

At the end Jobs seemed to have realized he needed to do more than work:

> "Jobs also prepared his personal legacy. In 2009, he finally started giving interviews to journalist Walter Isaacson to prepare for his first and only authorized biography, giving him his perspective on his life and career. He also spent his last days designing a boat for his family on which he hoped to travel the world. Unfortunately, death took him too soon, and he died peacefully at home on October 5, 2011, surrounded by his family—the day following the introduction of the iPhone 4S, an Apple event that he watched from his deathbed."[42]

Steve Jobs never took that trip around the world on his boat with his family; it was too late. A boat doesn't quite describe what Steve had planned to travel on; it was a spectacular yacht, the Venus.

The "Venus is a super yacht designed by Philippe Starck's design company Ubik and built by Feadship…the yacht was unveiled a year later at a cost of more than €100 million."[43]

It's difficult to even imagine such a grand vessel, yet Job's dream for this boat never happened. What about you? Is there something in your heart that is tugging at you? If it is in accordance with God's Word, then keep pressing toward it. God's dream for you will never go against His Word.

Each day is a gift from God; how are you spending it? Take time to smell the roses, coffee, and cookies in the oven. Be grateful for your senses. The most important things God has given us, we often take for granted. Think for a moment what you've been given and what you may take for granted. Don't miss it. It's easy to compare our lives to people who are the idols of our day, the folks whom Hollywood tells us we should aspire to be.

Do you think of your life as precious and important? It is. If you saw the movie *The Help*, you probably remember the famous line from the movie: "You is kind, you is smart, you is important." If you ever doubt this about yourself, you're telling yourself a lie. You're important no matter your age, your income, your family status, your health, or your present life situation.

My friend, believe again. Believe again that your life matters. Maybe it doesn't seem like it to you, and maybe those around you aren't telling you that it does, but it matters to God.

If you knew you were entering eternity in thirty days, what would you change? What would you do differently? Every day matters, and it can be hard to enjoy the present when you want change so badly and you're desperate for your life to be different.

Fame and fortune is not the answer, yet daily the social media and the array of ads throughout every form of advertising tell us differently. The talented Elvis Presley, Whitney Houston, and John Lennon are gone. Their lives ended in a tragic sad way. Not only does our world place so much notoriety on those who are musically talented, but also those who are gifted in sports. The article in *The Word for You Today*, December 29, 2015, issue, beautifully depicts why the pursuit of temporal and worldly successes in the end will not matter:

> Society's fascination with Hollywood and celebrities has gone a little crazy. Millions idolize those who have achieved fame and fortune, yet stardom does not provide the satisfaction it advertises. Marilyn Monroe could have told us that. So could Elvis Presley and Michael Jackson. Consider the adoration

accorded to Mohammed Ali in his prime. He was known as "the prize fighter who couldn't be beaten." His picture appeared on the cover of *Sports Illustrated* more than any other athlete in history. Wherever he went the cameras followed. But wealth and fame cannot buy good health, and he fell victim to the ravages of Parkinson's disease. Sportswriter Gary Smith spent some time with the ailing fighter at his home and asked to see his trophy room. Ali escorted him to a dark, damp barn beside his house. There, leaning against the wall was a board displaying mementoes – photos of the "Thrilla in Manila," pictures of Ali dancing and punching, and hoisting championship belts he had won over this head. But the pictures were smeared with white streaks caused by pigeons that had made their home in the rafters. Ali picked up the board and turned it around, face to the wall. Then as he started to leave, Smith heard him mumble, "I had the whole world, and it wasn't nuthin'. Look at me now." The Psalmist wrote, "All our busy rushing ends in nothing. We heap up wealth, not knowing who will spend it. And so, Lord, where do I put my hope? My only hope is in you" ([Psalm 39] vv 6-7 NLT)."[44]

We can learn a lot from those powerful few words Ali said, "I had the whole world and it wasn't nuthin." The pull the world has on us can be great. It's important not to let the tremendous fascination of the pleasures and the desire for worldly popularity creep into our hearts and mind. God says, "Do not love the world nor the things in the world. If anyone loves the world, the love of the Father is not in him" (1 John 2:15). This is a daily process. Our flesh will always be there. As you continue reading and studying God's Word, your hunger for Him will begin to outweigh your hunger for this world.

Did you see the movie *Heaven is for Real*, an "American Christian drama film, directed by Randall Wallace and written by Christopher Parker, based on Pastor Todd Burpo and Lynn Vincent's 2010 book of the same name?"[45] This powerful film and book tells the story about Todd Burro's near-death experience and his visit to heaven. Whether you're at a funeral, a graveyard, or watch the news of the brutal deaths that happen every single day, it's a part of life; someday we will all die.

The dash, that tiny mark between the dates on your tombstone, represents your life. And how you live that dash on your tombstone matters. It's my prayer that no matter where you are now, no matter what has happened—the disappointments, the discouraging setbacks— that you truly live life now. Painful, hurtful things may have wounded you deeply, but there is always hope and there's is a fresh exciting future for you.

Oh, I understand pain and deep disappointment. My life is drastically different than I had planned, yet I know God uses everything in our lives for good. I still trust and believe Him again and again and again. I know that God has a plan. Romans 8:28 is a simple, yet radically profound scripture that I stand on when the days are dark and challenging and I encourage you to do the same.

> "And we know that God causes all things to work together for good to those who love God, to those who are called according to *His* purpose"
> **—Romans 8:28**

God is in control, and I daily choose to believe God's purposes and plans are what is best. "The steps of a man are established by the Lord, And He delights in his way. When he falls, he will not be hurled headlong, Because the Lord is the One who holds his hand" (Psalm 37:23-24).

As you keep seeking the Lord through prayer and through the truth of His Word, He will direct how you are to live and where you are to go. Psalm 119:105 tells us, "Your word is a lamp to my feet And a light to my path."

One day all of us will step from this life to the next. I don't know if your time here is short or long, but no matter the length of time you have left, use it wisely. Risk more, love more, dream more, and believe more, and when you do, you will live more.

> Our greatest fear should not be of failure...but of succeeding at things in life that don't really matter.
> —**Francis Chan**

Step Ten: Live Again

1. Spend quality time really thinking and praying about what you would change if you had only thirty days to live.

2. Write a list of these things you desire to do and add them to your DREAM PLAN.

3. Are there people in your life you need to forgive? Is there anyone you need to write a letter to or get things right with? Do all that you can to be at peace with all men. God tells us to do this.

4. Do you have something you desire to do but you've been too scared to go after it? What risk can you begin taking to reach for that dream? Prayerfully seek God about moving forward.

5. Are you envious of others? Be honest with yourself and ask God to help you desire to make your life about "Reaching one more for Jesus." When your true aim in life becomes the Gospel of Jesus Christ, your outlook concerning others will dramatically change.

Prayer: Lord, forgive me for the countless hours I have wasted in my life. It's not my desire to continue to waste time. Lord, help me to always look for ways to reach one more for Jesus. If there is anyone whom

I possibly have not forgiven, show me who and how I can genuinely forgive them and make things right.

Help me risk more by running toward what You have uniquely designed me to do. I acknowledge that it is only through You that I can walk toward my dreams with boldness. Thank you in advance for what You are going to do.

Chapter 11

Finish Strong

Soar Again

… "Eye has not seen, nor ear heard,
Nor have entered into the heart of man
The things which God has prepared for those who love Him."
—1 Corinthians 2:9, NKJV

*H*ave you ever heard anyone call themselves a LOSER? Maybe they just put their hand in front of their forehead with fingers shaped like an *L* to indicate to you that they think they are a loser. I've seen people do this and, unfortunately, they meant it.

I'm glad that term wasn't trendy when I was an adolescent, but it's popular today. Loser is a terrible way for anyone to think about themselves. Merriam Webster defines the word, "Loser: a person or thing that loses especially consistently; a person who is incompetent or unable to succeed; *also*: something doomed to fail or disappoint."[46]

It's sad that anyone believes they are *doomed to fail*, yet some think this way. Do you recall the old cartoon "Popeye the Sailor Man"? John Ortberg writes in his book *The Life You've Always Wanted* about Popeye: "Popeye was not a sophisticated guy. He had never been in therapy and was woefully out of touch with his shadow self and his inner child. He did not have much education as far as we know. He knew who he was: a simple, sea-faring, pipe-smoking, Olive Oyl-loving sailor-man and he wouldn't pretend to be anything else. He 'owned his story,' as Lewis Smedes puts it. 'I yam what I yam.'

"But I always thought there was a note of sadness in Popeye's expression. It was generally offered as an explanation of his shortcomings. It does not anticipate much growth or change. It doesn't leave him much of a getting to be what he yam not. 'Don't get your hopes up,' he seemed to say. 'Don't expect too much. I yam what I yam—and [he would add in his bleakest moments] that's all that I yam. That is a sad cry of the human race. You have said those words, in your own way, and so have I. This is the struggle between disappointment and hope."[47]

Through Popeye, Ortberg gives us the perfect picture of how we can act or think if we're not careful. But it's such a huge lie if you're a Christian. You are *complete in Christ*, (Colossians 2:9-10), not a failure at all. There's always hope! Never lose hope—hope in Christ and in what He is calling you to. He has given you all your many gifts and talents unlike anyone else. You must believe *this* and not the lie of being a loser. It's important that you understand who you are in Christ—what He says about you in His Word. Then you won't depend on your own successes or failures but on His strength and power to lead and guide you far beyond your wildest dreams.

Unfortunately, too many are striving for success in every other way possible. Pushing, climbing, stretching, searching, and doing all they can to reach their dreams. As Christians we must do our part, but it's *in Christ* that makes all the difference. In Christ you were made for more. You were made to soar, no matter your physical limitations! Many don't understand who they really are in Christ and what God can do in and through their lives.

I will never forget the first time I heard this story. It illustrates beautifully how critical it is to understand who you really are.

You Were Made to Soar!

There's an old, well-known story of a chicken farmer who found an eagle's egg.

He put it with his chickens and soon the egg was hatched.

The young eagle grew up with all the other chickens and whatever they did, the eagle did too. He thought he was a chicken, just like them.

Since the chickens could only fly for a short distance, the eagle also learned to fly a short distance.

He thought that was what he was supposed to do. So that was all that he thought he could do. As a consequence, that was all he was able to do.

One day the eagle saw a bird flying high above him. He was very impressed. "Who is that?" he asked the hens around him.

"That's the eagle, the king of the birds," the hens told him. "He belongs to the sky. We belong to the earth; we are just chickens."

So the eagle lived and died as a chicken, for that's what he thought he was.

—Author unknown

Far too many are living in the dirt just like the chickens in this story. You may be living in sin, living in depression, darkness, dependent on everything else except Christ and Christ alone. You don't have to! You are not like the chickens! You were made to soar like the eagles!

Having a great career can often lead to having all the comforts that this life can bring—but all your stuff will not last. I'm passionate about telling everyone to dream big, soar like an eagle, and live life to the fullest. But I'm more passionate about people knowing that without Christ, nothing in this life really matters.

Have you known family and friends who, in an instant, discovered they had cancer, had a heart attack, or were in a horrible car accident—and lost their careers? Life as they knew it dramatically changed. What did they do? Where did they turn? Walking toward your God-given dreams is important, but it's more important to walk in Christ, live a Spirit-filled life, and do what He has called you to do.

I first talked about this in Chapter 1—it's not what you're doing, it's who you're becoming that matters. We're nothing apart from Him.

"'I am the vine, you are the branches; he who abides in Me and I in him, he bears much fruit, for apart from Me you can do nothing'" (John 15:5). If you remember anything from this book, remember this. You want to bear much fruit and have a life that matters by staying close to Jesus Christ and clinging to Him.

We're nothing without Him, but we're everything in Him! Let's look at just some of the things that you have when you are in Christ:

1. **You are a brand-new person.**
   Therefore if anyone is in Christ, he is a new creature; the old things passed away; behold, new things have come (2 Corinthians 5:17).

2. **You are no longer a slave to sin.**

   Even so consider yourselves to be dead to sin, but alive to God in Christ Jesus (Romans 6:11).

3. **You will forever live with Christ.**

   For the wages of sin is death, but the free gift of God is eternal life in Christ Jesus our Lord (Romans 6:23).

4. **You have His power living in you.**

   Therefore I am well content with weaknesses, with insults, with distresses, with persecutions, with difficulties, for Christ's sake; for when I am weak, then I am strong (2 Corinthians 12:10).

5. **You have the mind of Christ.**

   FOR WHO HAS KNOWN THE MIND OF THE LORD, THAT HE WILL INSTRUCT HIM? But we have the mind of Christ (1 Corinthians 2:16).

6. **You have the Holy Spirit living in you.**

   But if the Spirit of Him who raised Jesus from the dead dwells in you, He who raised Christ Jesus from the dead will also give life to your mortal bodies through His Spirit who dwells in you (Romans 8:11).

7. **You will never be separated from His love.**

   But in all these things we overwhelmingly conquer through Him who loved us. For I am convinced that neither death, nor life, nor angels, nor principalities, nor things present, nor things to come, nor powers, nor height, nor depth, nor any other created thing, will be able to separate us from the love of God, which is in Christ Jesus our Lord (Romans 8:37-38).

8. **You can have His peace.**

   And the peace of God, which surpasses all comprehension, will guard your hearts and your minds in Christ Jesus (Philippians 4:7).

9. **You are given eternal life.**

"For God so loved the world, that He gave His only begotten Son, that whoever believes in Him shall not perish, but have eternal life" (John 3:16).

10. **You are complete.**

For in Him all the fullness of Deity dwells in bodily form, and in Him you have been made complete, and He is the head over all rule and authority (Colossians 2:9-10).

These are just some of the many wonderful truths about being in Christ Jesus. It's important that you know these key promises as you press toward your God-given dreams.

As you seek God and have a clear vision of what He has called you to do, press forward and don't look back. Throughout Scripture you see ordinary people doing extraordinary things for God. They passionately ran toward God and what He called them to do.

Oh my friend, what's stopping you from pressing toward your dreams with all your heart? Have you tried and you're tired? Do you feel like you're getting nowhere? Oh, how I understand that it can be challenging at times. But *don't give up—continue to look up!* Keep believing again and again and again.

Are you afraid of your past or do your present circumstances hinder you from God's plans for your life? Just take the next step—and then keep walking! That's what Thelma Wells did despite her daunting upbringing. In Karol Ladd's book *Positive Leadership Principles for Women*, she writes about the way Thelma soared above the circumstances that could have crippled her life:

Thelma Wells is known for her smile, her candor, and her hope-infused messages to women. She was one of the first black women executives in the banking industry; in the following years she has become known worldwide as a Woman of Faith speaker, conference leader, and popular author. But her life hasn't always been an easy road to success. Her mother was an unwed teenager in a day when it was considered shameful to be pregnant and not married. Her maternal grandmother would not allow Thelma and her mom to stay in her home, so they lived in servants' quarters in a house in Dallas.

Thelma remembers visiting her grandmother's home as a little girl and being put in the closet—a dark, dingy, insect-infested closet—yet it was here that she began to sing the songs she remembered from church. Songs like "Amazing Grace" and "The Old Rugged Cross." Here in this dark dungeon, she felt closeness to God. She said, "I would sing myself to sleep with church songs. I had no bitterness, no anger, no strife, no malice, and no fear." What a picture of God hiding His children under the shadow of His wings![48]

Thelma is a dear friend, and I have never seen her when she did not radiate God's love toward others. She has used all the broken pieces of her life to help encourage countless others who are hurting and need reassurance that God does care.

In 1 Corinthians 9:24, Paul compares living our lives with running a race. He describes how we should run: "Do you not know that those who run in a race all run, but *only* one receives the prize? Run in such a way that you may win." What's your story? What's your deepest hunger and passion in life? No matter your age, you haven't finished running your race. This life is a marathon—not a quick sprint.

Don't you love watching the Olympics! What I have noticed through all the years of observing these incredible games is that the athletes all appear to have one thing in common: passion! They are passionate about winning, they are passionate about their sport, and they are passionate about helping their country win the most coveted medal—gold! Their discipline is outstanding, their focus is superb, and their commitment is unmatched. As Christians, we should have a passion and devotion to God above anyone and everything else.

Paul said, "Now they *do it* to obtain a perishable crown, but we *for* an imperishable *crown*" (1 Corinthians 9:25b, NKJV). We should have even greater passion than our Olympians have! We are a part of a royal priesthood! It's normal at times to miss this because of all the demands that this life can bring. It's easy to get your eyes off the prize and off of why you are here. God says this about you:

> But you are A CHOSEN RACE, a royal PRIESTHOOD, A HOLY NATION, A PEOPLE FOR *God's* OWN POSSESSION, so that you may proclaim the excellencies of Him who has called you out of darkness into His marvelous light; for you once were NOT A PEOPLE, but now you are THE PEOPLE OF GOD; you had NOT RECEIVED MERCY, but now you have RECEIVED MERCY.
> **—1 Peter 2:9-10**

Ask God to continue to grow your passion toward what He has called you to do. There is power in passion!

The Power of Passion

"Experts" spend a lot of time trying to figure out what makes people successful, and more than anything else, passion is what makes the difference.[49]

If that longing in your heart does not go away, it's your passion. If money were not an obstacle and you could do what you long to do, it's your passion. If you knew that no matter what time of day it was, you would wake up daily to do this, it's your passion.

If your sole purpose is about impacting others for Christ, then you have the correct motive for fulfilling your God-given passionate dreams.

What are you passionate about? You've seen in this book and know in your heart that God created you for this mission, for this purpose. You were created to soar and you were made for more. He has truly given you all that you need.

> ...His divine power has granted to us everything pertaining to life and godliness, through the true knowledge of Him who called us by His own glory and excellence.
> **—2 Peter 1:3**

You have everything you need for life and godliness through Jesus Christ! Don't you love that!

God may be molding you and preparing you for much more than you could ever imagine. "...He who has begun a good work in you will complete *it* until the day of Jesus Christ" (Philippians 1:6, NKJV). God will finish what He starts! Today it may be awfully dark for you, but *God is there, and He will help you!*

Remember Joseph? If you don't know the story, I would encourage you to read and study his life in Genesis 37–50. Joseph went from a pit to a palace, and he had a lot of enormous hardships in between! Over and over he was wrongfully treated, and he could easily have given up on God and everyone around him. *Yet,* he believed God time and time again, even when his circumstances looked discouraging and depressing.

Joseph's unwavering faith, his incredible focus, and his consistent belief that God had allowed all the difficult hardships in his life for a reason were simply amazing. In Genesis 50:16-21, we see how Joseph responded to his brothers who had left him for dead in a pit when he was a young man. But years later, Joseph was in charge and ruled over Egypt. He could easily have gotten even—instead, read what he did:

> So they sent *a message* to Joseph, saying, "Your father charged before he died, saying, 'Thus you shall say to Joseph, "Please forgive, I beg you, the transgression of your brothers and their sin, for they did you wrong."'" And now, please forgive the transgression of the servants of the God of your father." And Joseph wept when they spoke to him. Then his brothers also came and fell down before him and said, "Behold, we are your servants." But Joseph said to them, "Do not be afraid, for am I in God's place? As for you, you meant evil against me, *but* God meant it for good in order to bring about this present result, to preserve many people alive. So therefore, do not be afraid; I will provide for you and your little ones." So he comforted them and spoke kindly to them.

Joseph—oh, what a man of faith!

I don't know the difficult circumstances God has allowed in your life, but cling to His Word and to His promises that tell you that nothing can stop God's plan and purpose for your life. I don't know where you are in your journey, but God does. You may wish that you were out of that eagles' nest. It's possible that God still has you waiting before you fly for a reason known only to Him. But in the meantime, take the next step. Do something now. Often in time, little steps toward your God-given design can make a big difference.

> "I know that You can do all things,
> And that no purpose of Yours can be thwarted."
> **—Job 42:2**

Dare to believe God again and again and again! Step up and step out into the glorious great adventure God has planned for you! Do you see it? Can you imagine it? What's your heart whispering to you deep in your soul? Now begin boldly walking toward your God-given dreams!

Now to Him who is able to do far more abundantly beyond all that we ask or think, according to the power that works within us, to Him *be* the glory in the church and in Christ Jesus to all generations forever and ever. Amen.

—Ephesians 3:20-21

Step Eleven: Soar Again

As you consider your new future, walk boldly with confidence toward your God-given dreams. This book was written purposely with eleven easy-to-remember steps—steps that will take you toward a new tomorrow if you earnestly seek God and move daily toward the unimaginable life He has planned for you.

Today Will You Boldly

1. Believe Again
2. Stand Again
3. Dream Again
4. Be Fearless Again
5. Fight Again
6. Purpose Again
7. Move Again
8. Plan Again
9. Wait Again
10. Live Again
11. Soar Again

My prayer for you is that today will be a new beginning for you. Wherever you are on your journey, keep going and keep growing! No matter your age, young or old, God desires to use you in a big way. Aim high, and soar above all the storms, above all the naysayers, and above anything you ever dreamed or imagined. Dare to believe again!

About the Author

Kathleen Hardaway is an author and a national speaker with a passion to encourage and equip people to live out their God-given dreams. She exhorts her audiences to dream big, never give up, and live an audacious life through Christ.

Kathleen has been a featured guest on Daystar Television, the NRB Network, and other nationally syndicated television programs. She's been on Moody Radio's *Midday Connection*, Dr. Gary Chapman's *Building Relationships,* and many other radio broadcasts. She is also the author of *I Kissed a Lot of Frogs, But the Prince Hasn't Come.*

Kathleen was on staff at Precept Ministries International for over 30 years. Kathleen has seen the power of God's Word change the lives of millions throughout the globe who study the Bible inductively and who choose to walk according to God's principles.

She has served ten years on the Board of Christian Women in Media Association and has worked as a director and producer for Christian programing for over twenty-five years.

Kathleen speaks with passion, humor, and biblical truths on relevant topics that touch audiences of all ages. She travels nationally and internationally with her heart-felt message of hope and encouragement.

She challenges her audience to "Dare to believe God for the impossible!"

For more information about Kathleen and her "Dare to Believe Again" seminars, visit her website at www.kathleenhardaway.com.

Acknowledgements

I can't imagine my life without the love and support of my family and friends. Thank you, mom, for always being there and supporting me throughout my God-sized dreams. The list is too long to name the vast number of people who have helped encourage me to live my God-given dreams.

I would like to acknowledge my DREAM TEAM; without them this book probably would never have been written. When the many disappointments knocked on my door, these women prayed, listened, encouraged, and helped me to press on. My deepest heartfelt gratitude to Jan Jeter, Robin Bertram, Karol Ladd, Dianne Williams, and the late Annette Garcia.

I would also like to thank the women who are not only dear friends, but gifted editors and proof readers: Carolyn Capp, Joye Howard, Paula Ewing. Thank you for helping me to make this book a reality.

Thank you Billy Graham, Kay Arthur, Joni Eareckson Tada, Anne Graham Lotz, Priscilla Shirer, and Beth Moore. It's hard to comprehend how different my life might have been without these wonderful people who heard God's call on their lives and followed Him passionately. Our world has greatly been impacted for good by these spiritual giants.

Endnotes

1   "Survey Finds Continued Worker Discontent," Right Management Man Power Groups, November 27, 2012, accessed September14. 2014, http://www.right.com/news-and-events/press-releases/2012-press-releases/item24318.aspx.

2   *Gravity* (film), *Wikipedia*, accessed September 14, 2014, http://en.wikipedia.org/wiki/Gravity_(film).

3   "Gravity, Venice Review," Hollywood Reporter, August 28, 2013, accessed September 14, 2014, http://www.hollywoodreporter.com/movie/gravity/review/615139.

4   "Gallup says 70% of Americans negative about their jobs...," Dealer Refresh, June 25, 2013, accessed August 20, 2014, http://forum.dealerrefresh.com/f40/gallup-says-70-americans-negative-about their-jobs-3415.html.

5   Andy Stanley, *Visioneering*, (Sisters, Oregon: Multnomah Publishers, Inc., 1999), 225.

6   "*Chariots of Fire*," *Wikipedia*, accessed August 25, 2014, http://
    en.wikipedia.org/wiki/Chariots_of_Fire.

7   Ibid.

8   "Chariots of Fire (1981) Quotes," IMDb, http://www.imdb.com/
    title/tt0082158/quotes.

9   "Angel Tree Celebrates 30 Years," Prison Fellowship, accessed
    September 2, 2014, http://www.prisonfellowship.org/story/
    angel-tree-celebrates-30-years/.

10 "Mary Kay Beard," *Bhamwiki*, last modified April 22. 2016,
    accessed May, 2016, http://www.bhamwiki.com/w/Mary_Kay_
    Beard.
    (During the writing of this book, Mary Kay Beard passed from
    this life into the presence of the Lord on Sunday, April 17, 2016.
    You may read her obituary at http://www.newstribune.com/
    obits/2016/apr/20/mary-kay-beard/53388/.)

11 Colonel Harland Sanders, Biography, accessed August 5, 2014,
    http://colonelsanders.com/bio.asp.

12 Nick Vuijicic, *Life Without Limits*, (Colorado Springs, CO: Water
    Brook Press, 2010), vii.

13 Ibid.

14 "Christopher Columbus," *Wikipedia*, accessed on November 11,
    2014, http://en.wikipedia.org/wiki/Christopher_Columbus.

15 "Christopher Columbus Quotes," Brainy Quote, accessed on
    November 12, 2014, http://www.brainyquote.com/quotes/
    authors/c/christopher_columbus.html.

16 "Todd Beamer," *Wikipedia*, accessed on November 12, 2014,
    http://en.wikipedia.org/wiki/Todd_Beamer.

17 Henry Ford, *Wikiqote*, accessed September 4, 2014, http://
    en.wikiquote.org/wiki/Henry_Ford.

18 Cliff Hollingsworth and Akiva Goldsman: *The Shooting Script:
    Cinderella Man*, (NewYork: Newmarket Press, 2005), xiii.

19 Ibid., x.

20 Ibid., 40.

21 Lysa TerKeurst, *Radically Obedient, Radically Blessed*, (Harvest House Publishers: Eugene, OR, 2003), 10.

22 "Bernard Madoff," *Wikipedia*, accessed August 19, 2014, http://en.wikipedia.org/wiki/Bernard_Madoff.

23 Stormie Omartian, *Just Enough Light for the Step I'm On*, (Eugene, OR: Harvest House Publishers,1999),

24 "Procrastination," *Wikipedia* accessed December 23, 2014, http://en.wikipedia.org/wiki/Procrastination.

25 "Chronic Stress is Linked to the Six Leading Causes of Deaths," Miami Herald.com, accessed December 22, 2014, http://www.miamiherald.com/living/article1961770.html.

26 "Abraham Lincoln," *Wikipedia*, accessed December 23, 2014, http://en.wikipedia.org/wiki/Abraham Lincoln.

27 Perfectionism (psychology), *Wikipedia*, accessed December 28, 2014, http://en.wikipedia.org/wiki/Perfectionism_%28psychology%29.

28 "Mary Kay Ash," *Wikipedia*, accessed December 28, 2014, https://en.wikipedia.org/wiki/Mary_Kay_Ash.

29 "Mary Kay," *Wikipedia*, accessed December 28, 2014, http://en.wikipedia.org/wiki/Mary_Kay.

30 Ibid., "Mary Kay Ash."

31 "Focus," *Merriam-Webster*, accessed September 25, 2014, http://www.merriam-webster.com/dictionary/focus.

32 George Sweeting, *Too Soon to Quit*, (Chicago, IL: Moody Publishing,1999), 21.

33 "The Life of Howard G. "Prof" Hendricks," DTS.edu, accessed July 11, 2015, http://www.dts.edu/read/howard-hendricks-prof/.

34 "Martin Luther King Jr. Quotes," BrainyQuote, accessed September 25, 2014, http://www.brainyquote.com/quotes/authors/m/martin_luther_king_jr.html.

35 "Ali Hafed," Bible.org, G. Sweeting, May, 1988, Moody Monthly, p. 95, accessed June 14, 2016, https://bible.org/illustration/ali-hafed.

36 "The Ray Kroc Story" McDonalds.com, accessed June 14, 2016, http://www.mcdonalds.com/us/en/our_story/our_history/the_ray_kroc_story.html.

37 Ibid.

38 "People Who Switched Their Careers after 50 (and Thrived)," Mental Floss, accessed June14, 2016, http://mentalfloss.com/article/24688/10-people-who-switched-careers-after-50-and-thrived.

39 Ibid.

40 "Puba," Wikipedia, accessed June 14, 2016, https://en.wikipedia.org/wiki/Pupa#Chrysalis.

41 "Pastor Rick Warren Shares Story of Fathers Final Words: Reach One More For Jesus," C P Church and Ministry, accessed December 29, 2015, http://www.christianpost.com/news/pastor-rick-warren-shares-story-of-fathers-final-dying-words-reach-one-more-for-jesus-126720/.

42 "Short Bio," All About Steve Jobs.com, accessed December 30, 2015, http://allaboutstevejobs.com/bio/shortbio.php.

43 "Venus (yacht)," Wikipedia, accessed January 20, 2015, https://en.wikipedia.org/wiki/Venus_(yacht).

44 "The Futility of Fame and Fortune," The Word for You Today, December January February, (Celebration, Inc., 2015) 19.

45 "Heaven Is for Real (film)," Wikipedia, accessed Dec 31, 2015, https://en.wikipedia.o rg/wiki/Heaven_Is_for_Real_(film).

46 "Loser," Merriam-Webster, accessed September 25, 2014, http://www.merriam-webster.com/dictionary/loser.

47 John Ortberg, *The Life You've Always Wanted*, (Grand Rapids, MI: Zondervan, 2002), 13-14.

48 Karol Ladd, *Positive Leadership Principles for Women*, (Eugene, OR: Harvest House Publishers, 2014), 77-78.

49 John Maxell, *Encouragement Changes Everything*, (Nashville, TN: Thomas Nelson, Inc., 2008), 116.

Morgan James makes all of our titles available through the Library for All Charity Organizations.

www.LibraryForAll.org

Printed in the USA
CPSIA information can be obtained
at www.ICGtesting.com
JSHW082350140824
68134JS00020B/1989